GROSSES BÊTES & PETITES BÊTES

(Big Beasts & Little Beasts)

Images and Text by
ANDRÉ HELLÉ

Published by SLG Publishing
44 Race Street
San Jose, CA 95126

www.slgpubs.com

isbn 978-1-59362-291-6

Author Bio

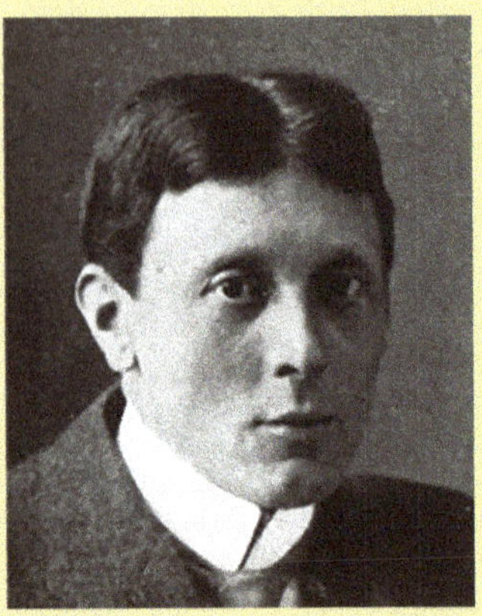

André Hellé was the pseudonym of André Laclôtre, a French painter and illustrator , lithographer and designer of very innovative wooden toys. Born in 1871 in Boissy-Saint-Leger, France Laclôtre assumed the pseudonym of André Hellé around 1896 when he began to publish drawings and comics in various magazines and other periodicals. In 1910, he began crafting models and wooden toys that were unique for the time and are still appealing. He produced a wooden toy series called "The Ark of Noah", most of the designs were later reused for the images in this book. He was awarded several awards for his toy designs. You only have to look at one of Helle's toy designs to see how much his style crossed over between the two worlds.

In addition to his popular children's books and illustration, André Hellé was also a noted satirist whose work appeared in a French newspaper called The Journal as well as several magazines including The Caricature (1900-1904), The Laughter (1901-1915) and The Parisian Life (1909-1920).

André Hellé's work had a very modern feel to it, minimal lines and shop edges and curves with simple, yet brilliant coloring. The work holds up well to this day and you would be hard-pressed to see this as a work from over a century ago.

His work is looked back on fondly to this day, especially in his hometown where the municipal library was named after him in 2015.

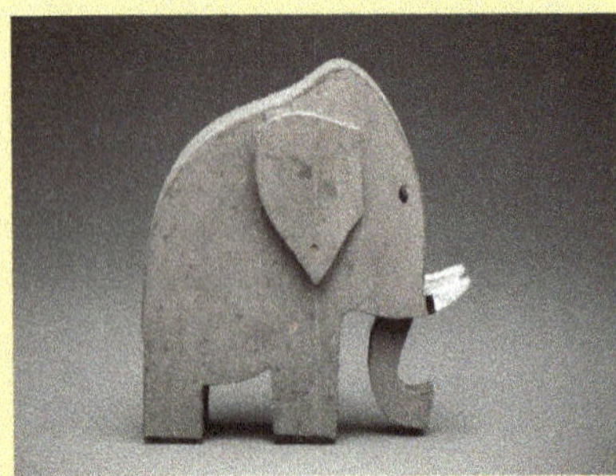

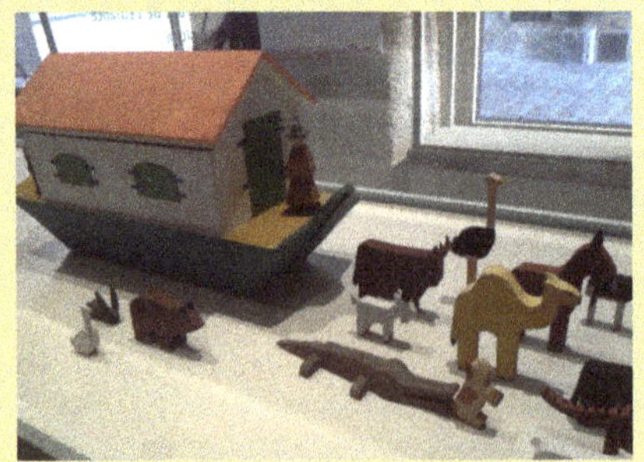

Photo courtesy CAROL GILLOTT
Used with permission

Editor's Notes

The book you are holding, Great Beasts and Small Beasts, was first published in the early 1900's and was one of Helle's better known children's books. While the art in the book is timeless and gorgeous, the text is, well, a bit dated. We attempted to translate this book (there is, to our knowledge, no English translation in existence) in a way that captured the spirit of the original book while making the passages both a little less archaic.

For instance in this book's literal translation from the original French, the Tiger is a beast to be feared and hunted. We changed that part a bit to reflect how tigers in the wild really live while still keeping the spirit of how the original book was written.

All of the art in the book was digitally traced from scan of the original book. Great care was taken to make sure the coloring and fine lines of the original artist were left intact while creating new artwork minus the fuzzy details and artifact-ridden color found in most reproductions of public domain works. The final product is as true to the original as we can get given the age and condition of the source material.

A note on the content of the book. Beyond some of the animal descriptions being dated, some of the images and text would be considered somewhat racist by today's standards. It was difficult for me, in pulling this project together, to decide to whether to keep the book as close to the original as possible, or remove the possibly offensive images. In the end I decided to keep the book intact visually while editing the text to try and better reflect our current values.

L'ARCHE DE NOÉ

(Noah's Ark)

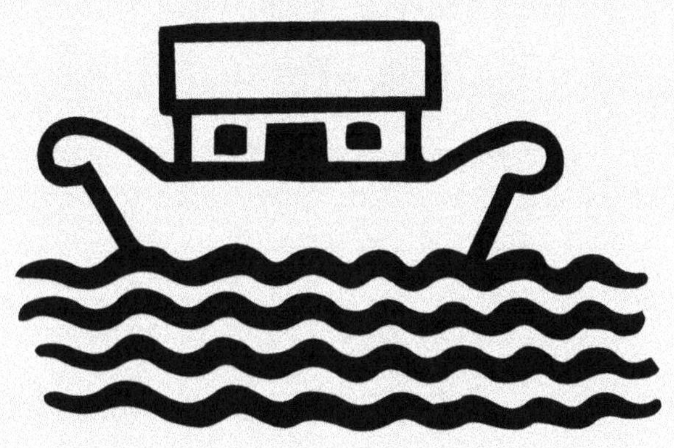

TABLE

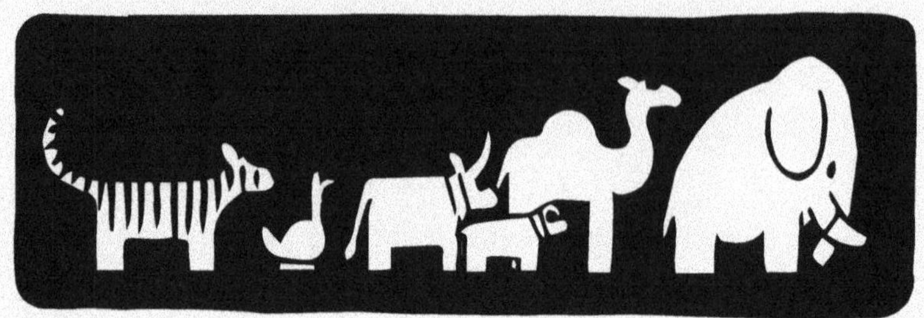

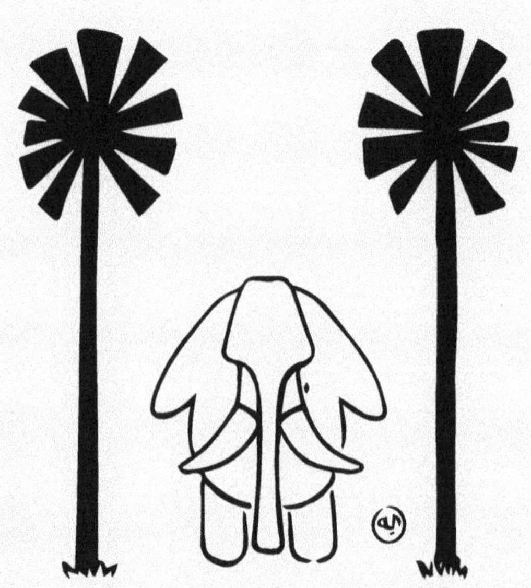

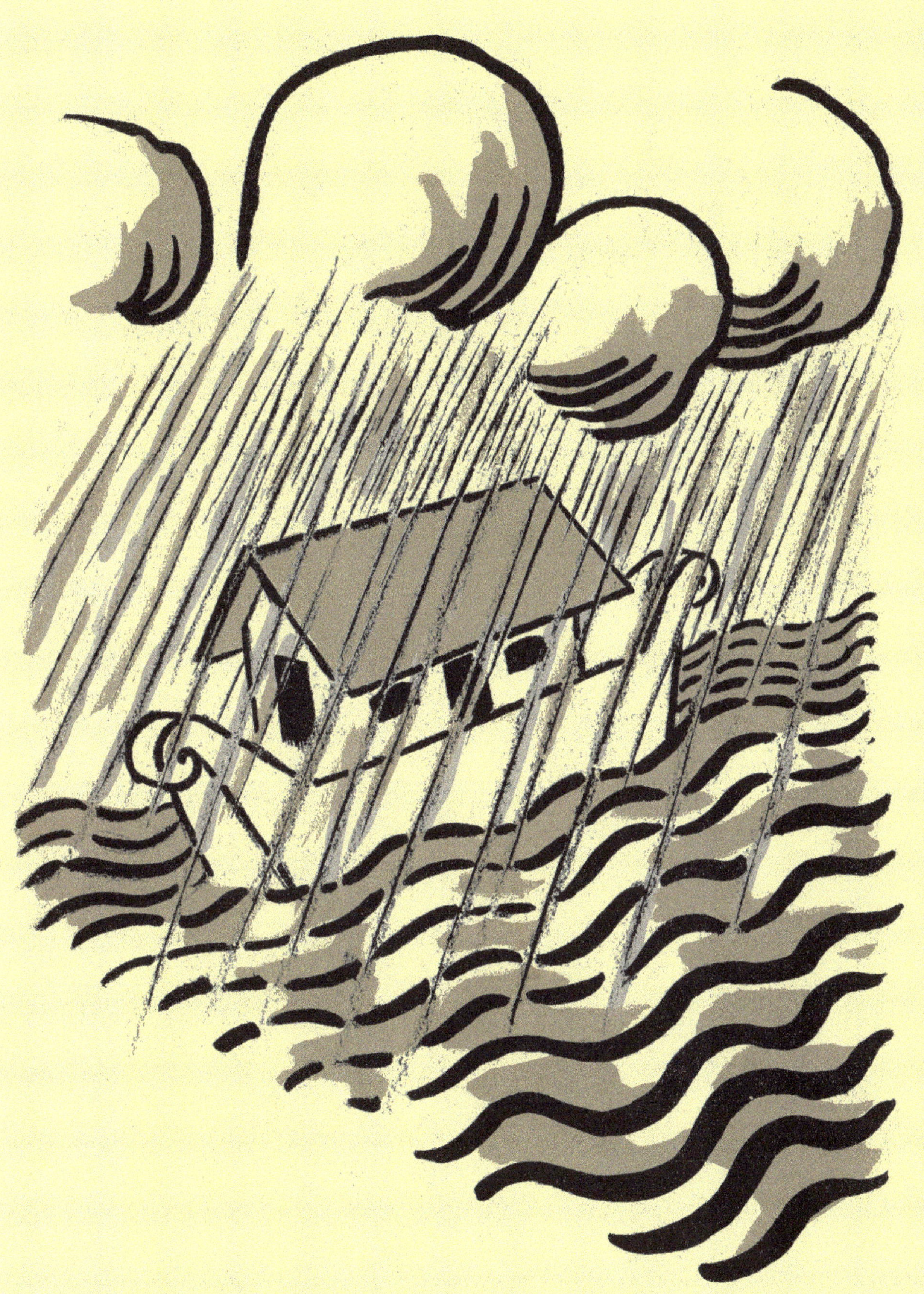

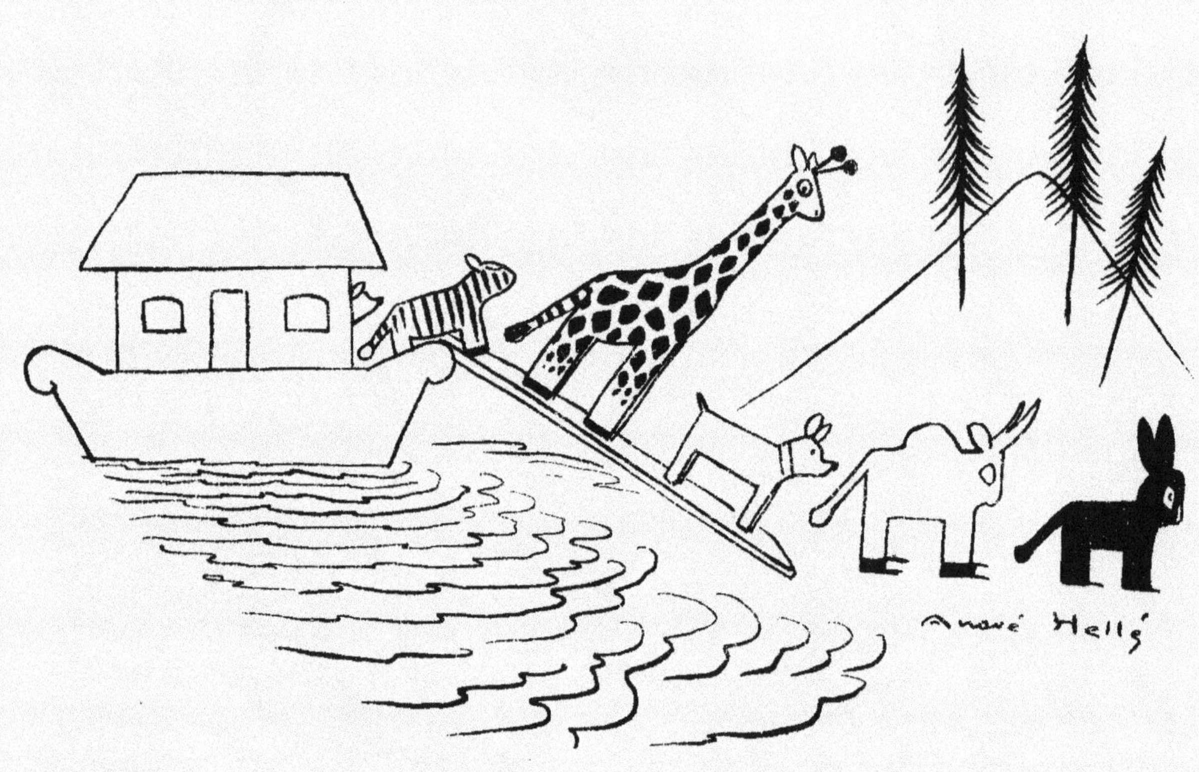
André Hellé

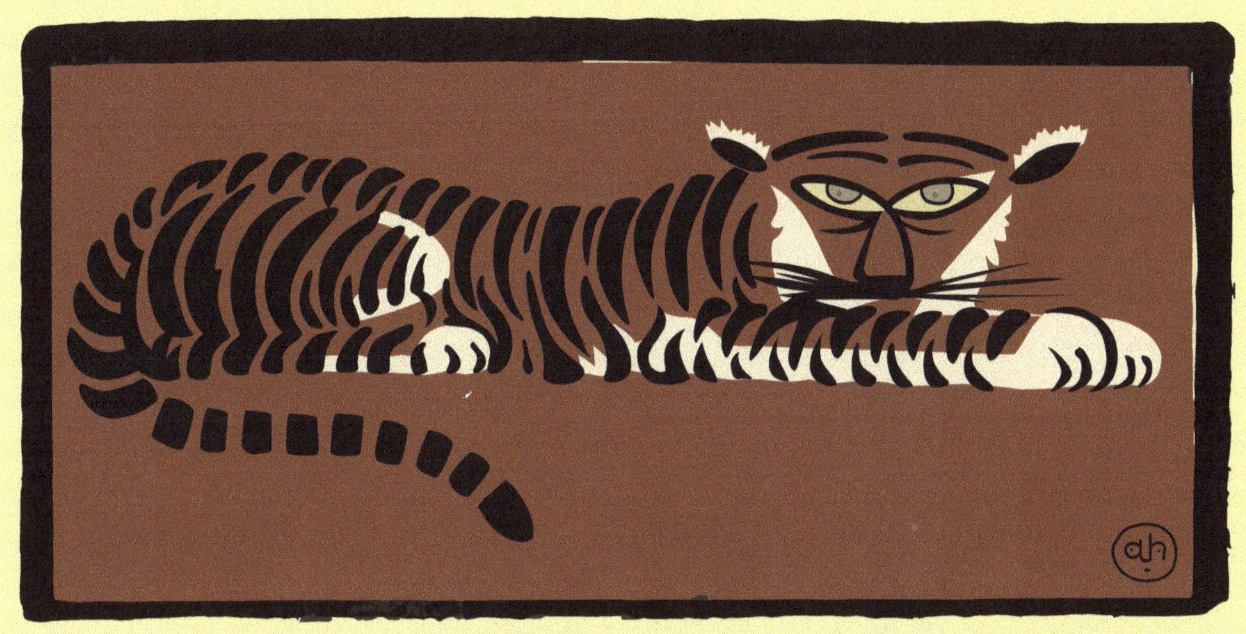

LE TIGRE

(The Tiger)

Yellow and black, with long whiskers that are sensitive to the touch, the tiger looks like a big orange and black tabby cat. But it is actually one of the fiercest creatures

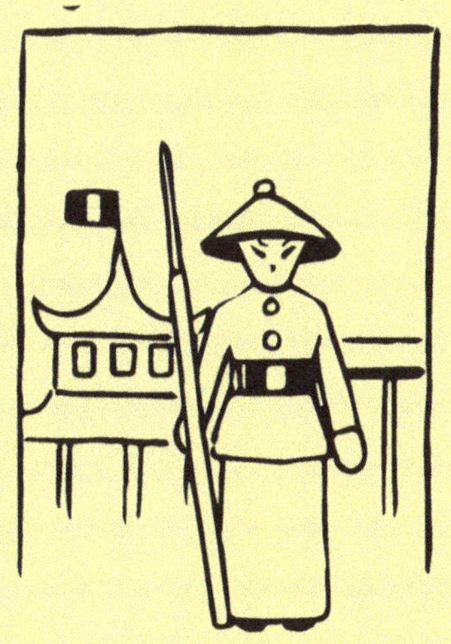

on the planet. It lives mostly in Southern Asia, with almost half of the world's population living in India.

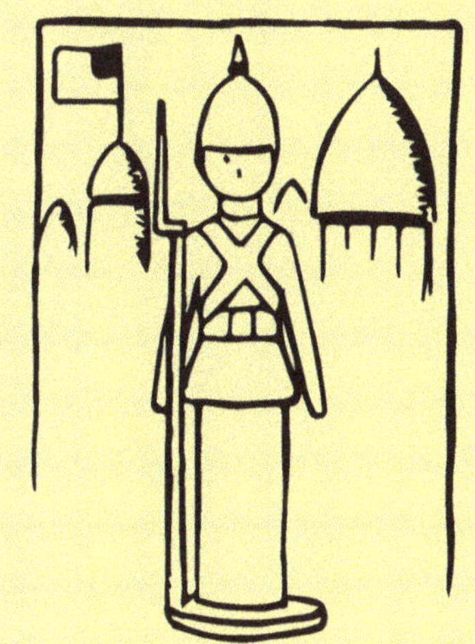

Tigers live where there are trees, bushes, and clumps of tall grass. This not only shades the Tiger from the extremely hot sun, but helps to camouflage them and surprise their prey. Stealthy and quiet, the tiger is a skilled hunter. The tiger seeks out buffalo or other large prey for its dinner.

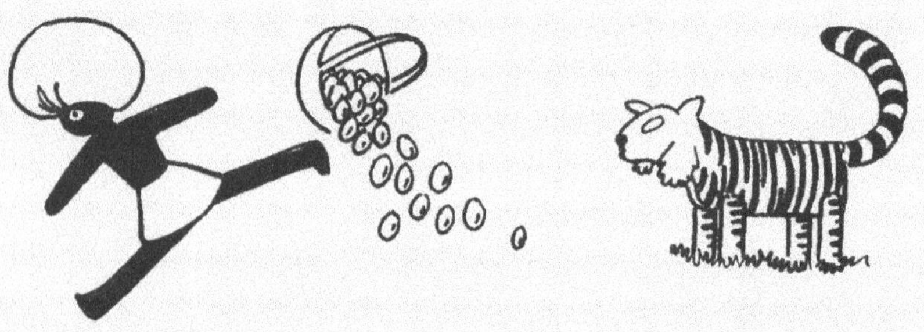

In some places the tiger is called a "maneater", yet, man hunts tiger more than tiger hunts man. Many an innocent tiger has found itself a trophy on a wall or a

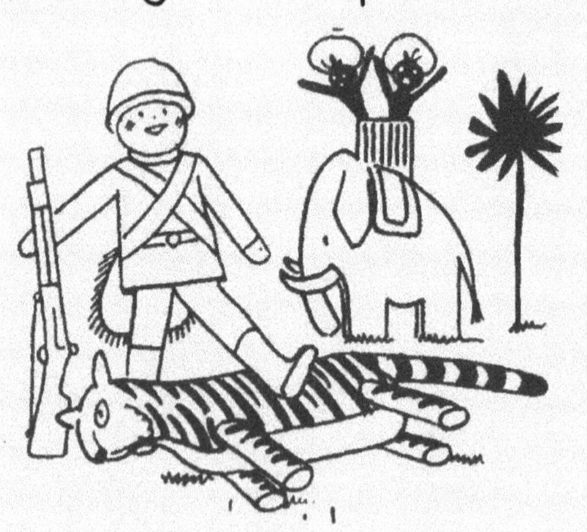

rug on a floor, killed for their pelts with little regard for their species survival. As mighty as the tiger is, the only beast it truly fears is man.

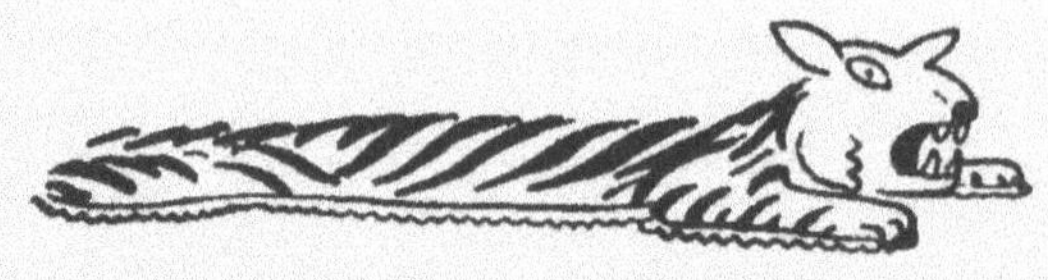

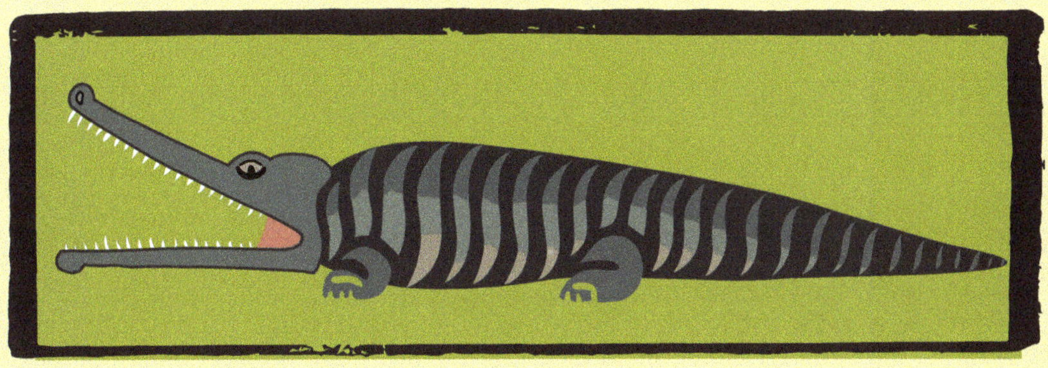

LE CROCODILE

(The Crocodile)

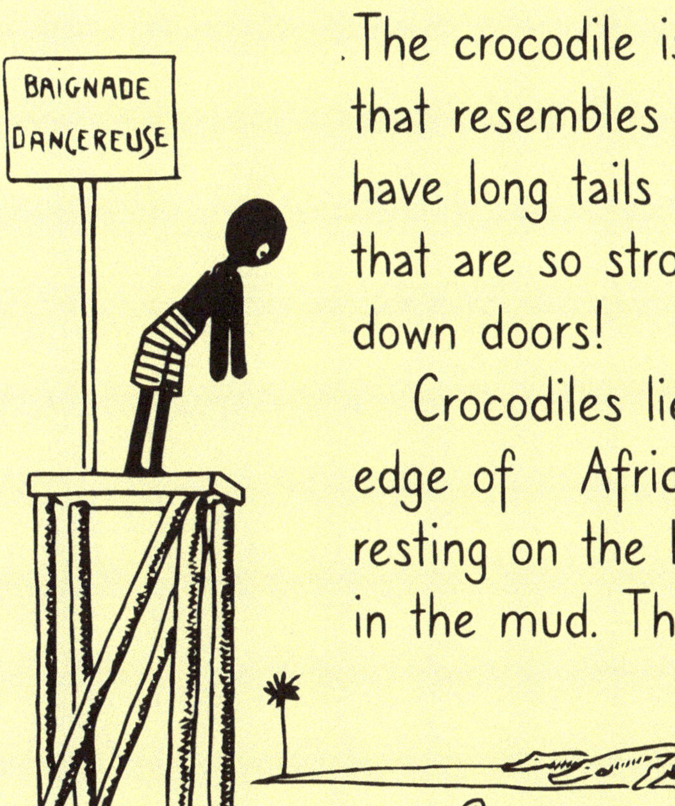

The crocodile is a hideous animal that resembles a large lizard. They have long tails used for swimming, that are so strong enough to break down doors!

Crocodiles lie dormant at the edge of Africa's largest rivers, resting on the banks or buried in the mud. They sit, waiting.

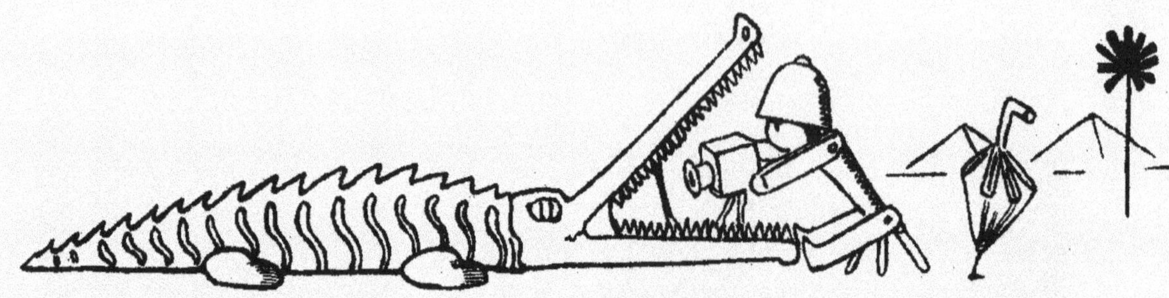

Crocodiles can sit for hours and hours, blending into the water and grass around them. Their coloring makes them look like fallen tree trunk, which allows them to easily sneak up on their dinner.

The crocodile's body is totally covered with scales, providing it with a hard shell that can protect it from bullets most things, sometimes even bullets. It cannot protect it, however, from people who want to turn their beautiful skins into shoes, suits and belts.

Its mouth is lined with sharp teeth. You should be careful around the mouth of a crocodile as it can easily swallow large animals.

They may be large and dangerous creatures, but when crocodiles eat too much, their stomachs get so big and full that they cannot move! Not even a step! They must fully digest their food before they can eat or hunt again.

LE DINDON

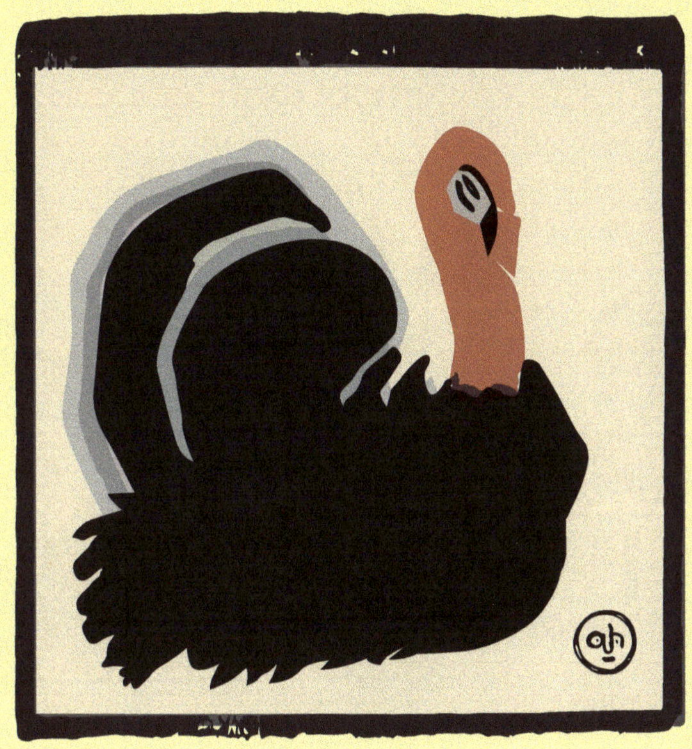

(The Turkey)

Wobbling through the fields, the turkey proudly shows its long black neck and glorious red crest. Why? Nobody knows. Though a member of the bird family, the turkey cannot fly very far. Sometimes it can flap its wings and lift slightly into the air, but it does not actually need to. All of the turkey's food conveniently grows on the ground.

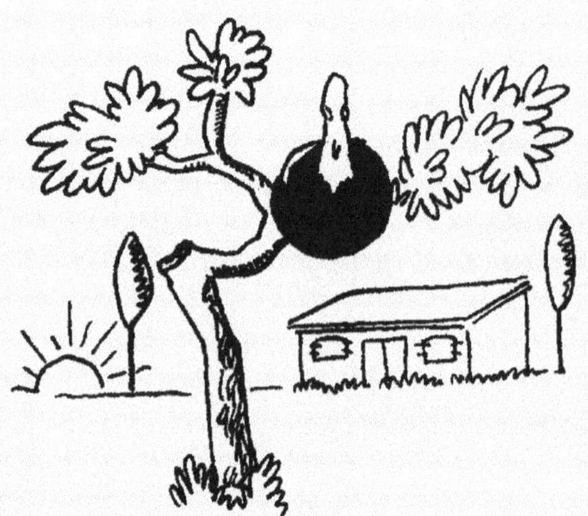

During the day the turkey loves to walk tall and make a variety of loud sounds.

Despite this, turkeys think they are very noble and important birds. Do you know why the turkey is so proud?

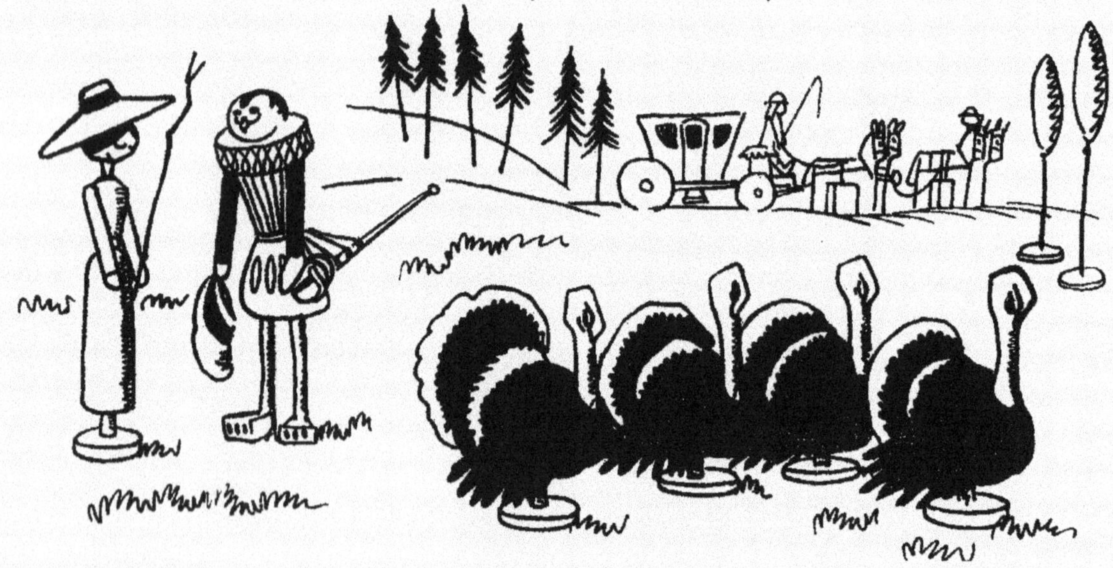

Long ago, in the time of fairy tales, the turkey was once protected and kept safe by castle guards. No one was to harm the turkeys, except for the kitchen cooks who could only kill them for special events. The turkey was then served to kings, queens, and the nobility as part of an impressive dinner!

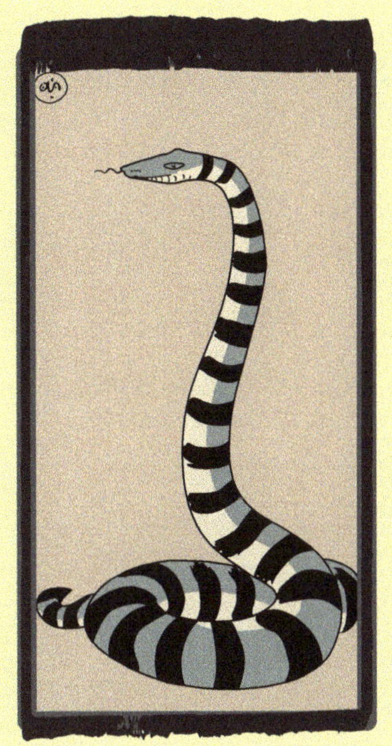

LE SERPENT

(The Snake)

The serpent (snake) is a reptile that prefers warmer climates. In such regions, the snake uses wood and old walls as a hiding places for the winter, while during the summer they can often be seen out in the open sunning themselves on rocks. Many snakes are poisonous.

Their bites are very strong and they store venom in their fangs.

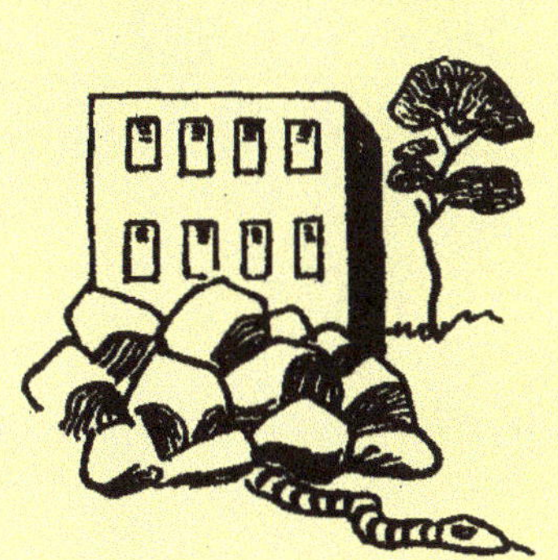

They mostly travel on the ground, but can also climb trees. While they do not have any legs, they are surprisingly fast and can climb very high. Some snakes like a Python are so big and strong that they can even eat large animals.

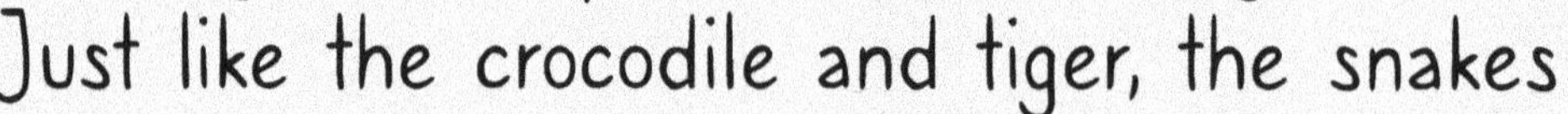

Just like the crocodile and tiger, the snakes use camouflage to help them hide. Snakes come in many different sizes and colors. Their scales provide a unique pattern and color for each species.

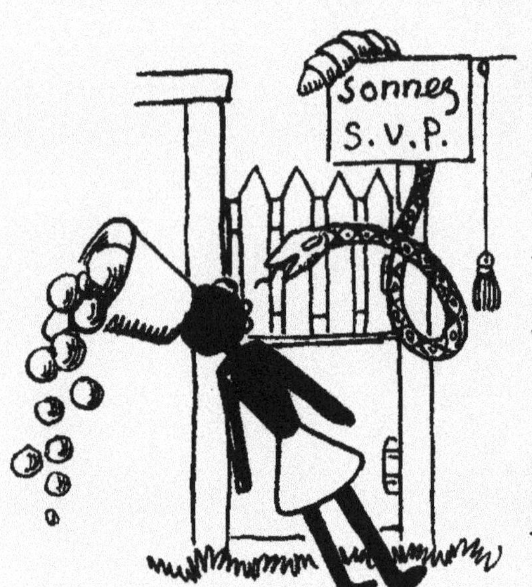

Although most snakes are poisonous, some are not. People try to tame the snakes and train them, though they are wild animals and are very hard to keep at home. So when you do see a snake, it is best to just leave it alone and walk away.

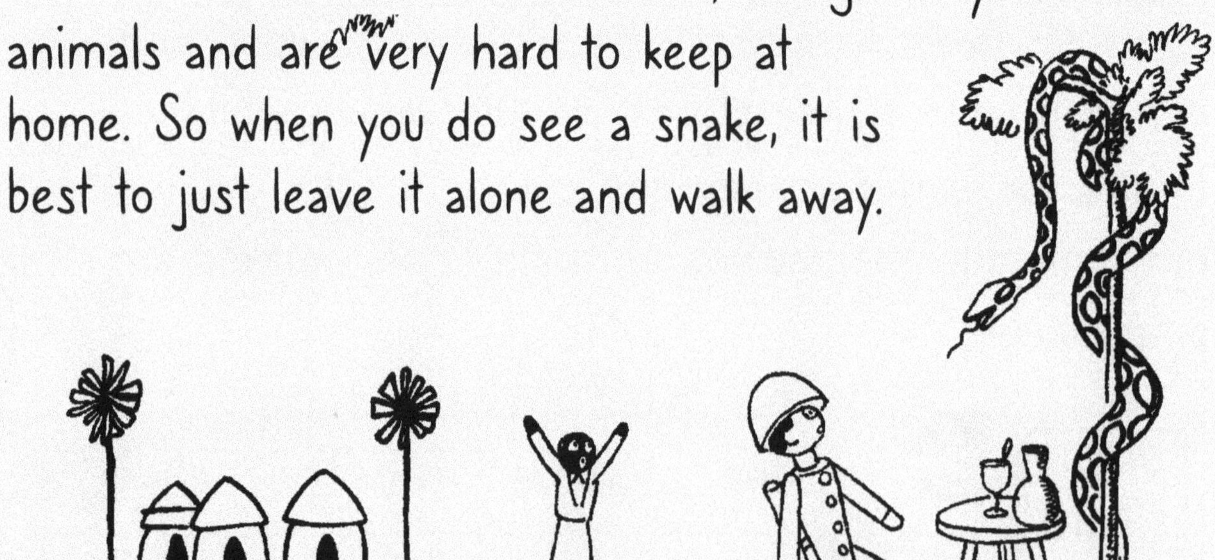

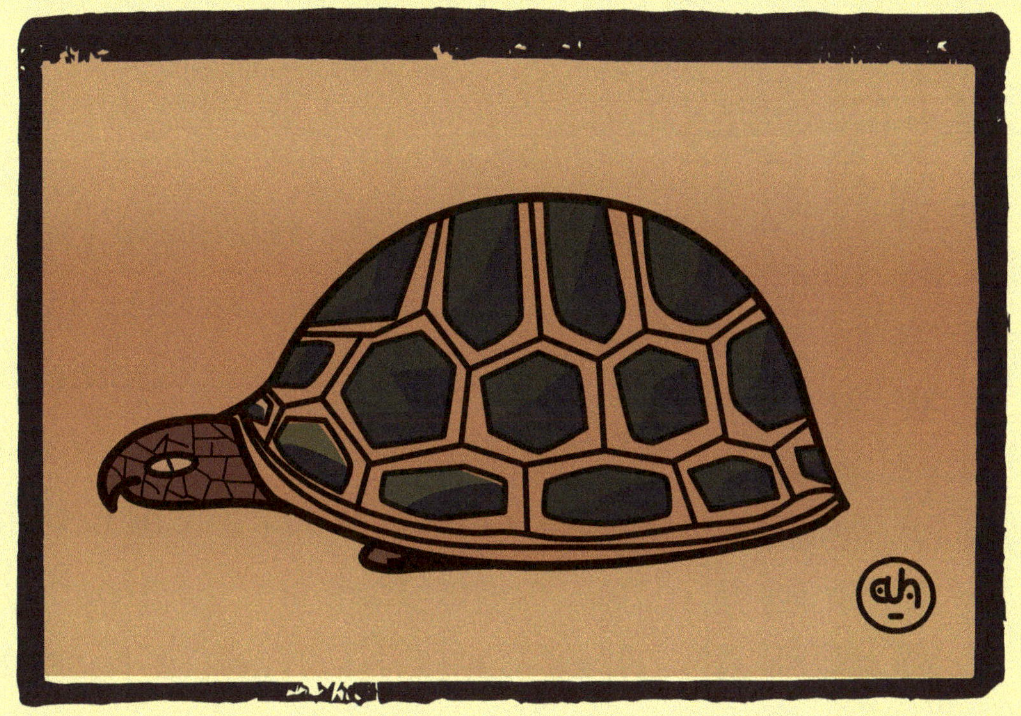

LA TORTUE

(The Turtle)

A member of the reptile family, the turtle has a very large shell covered by scales. This shell looks and feels a lot like bone, because it is one! That does not mean that the turtle has an exoskeleton, meaning their bones are on the outside of their body! The covering on a turtles shell is kind of like your own fingernail. When it senses danger, it hides in its shell.

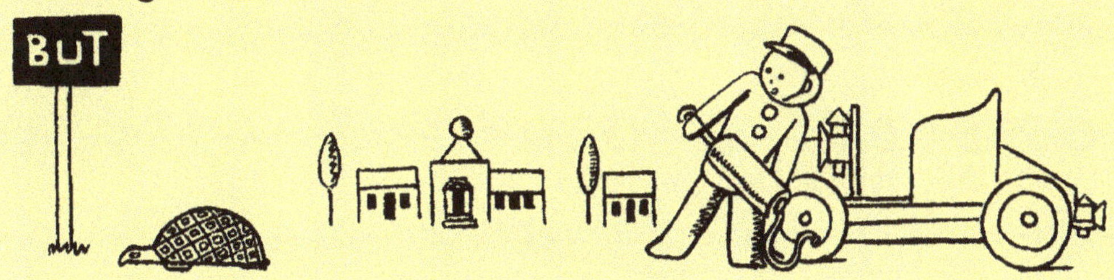

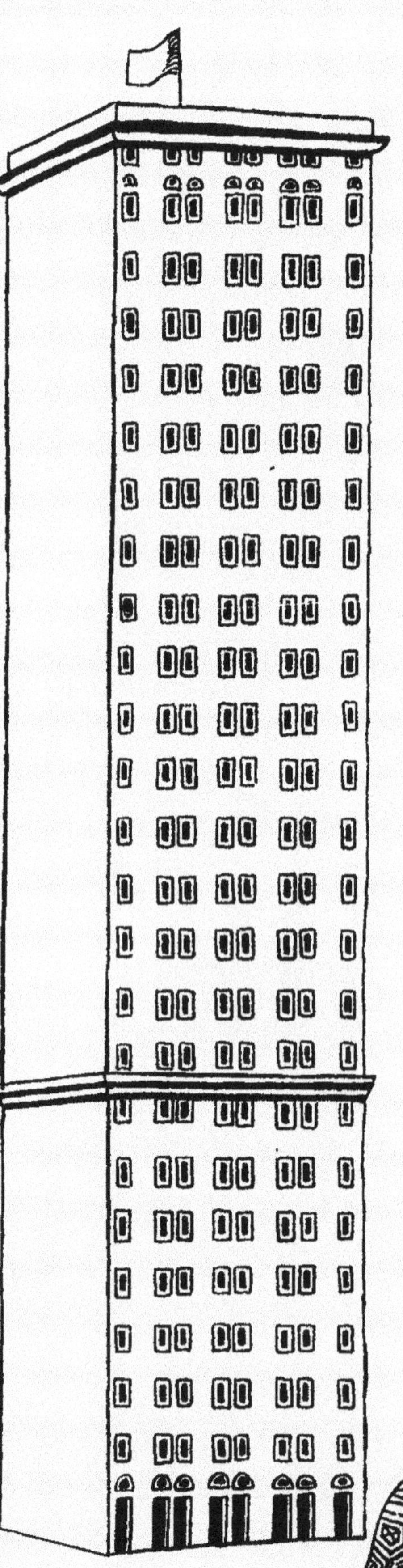

Though turtles are famously slow, it can be relatively fast when necessary. Turtles come in a variety of sizes. Some are huge, big enough that kids can ride on their backs. Then there are some that are so small that they could fit inside a baseball cap. Some of them live on the ground and others in the water. The fun thing to remember about the turtle is that its shell is its home, just like a snail. However, if you were to compare them, the turtle's shell is like a mansion compared to a snail's. The turtle can travel all over the world and never leave his home behind.

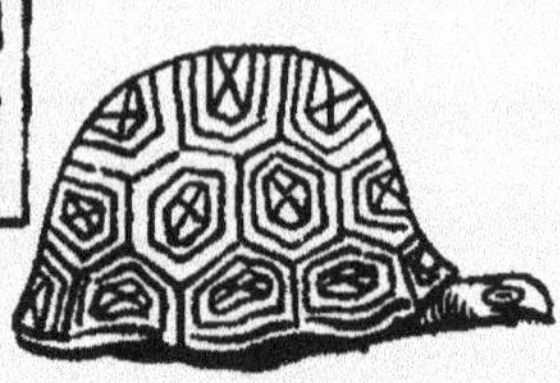

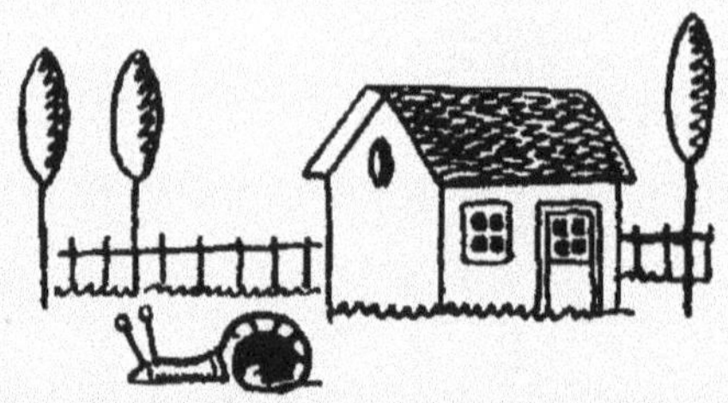

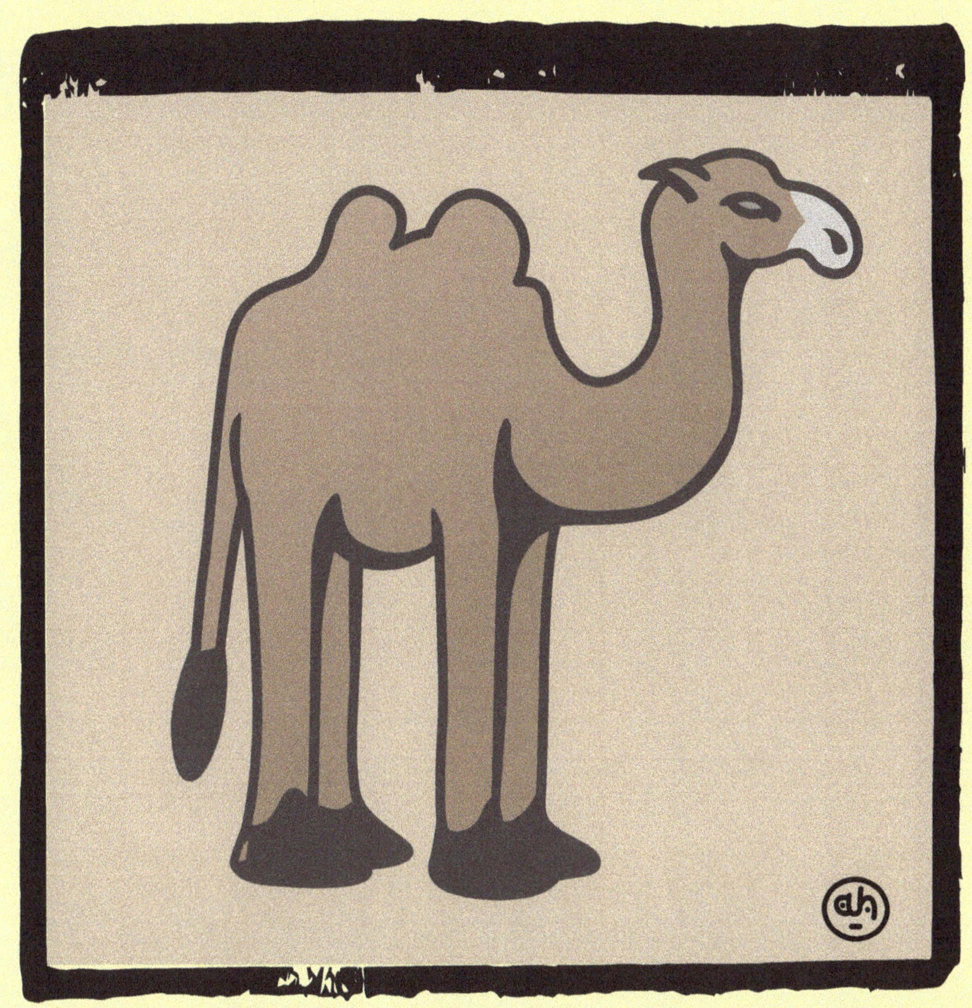

LE CHAMEAU

(The Camel)

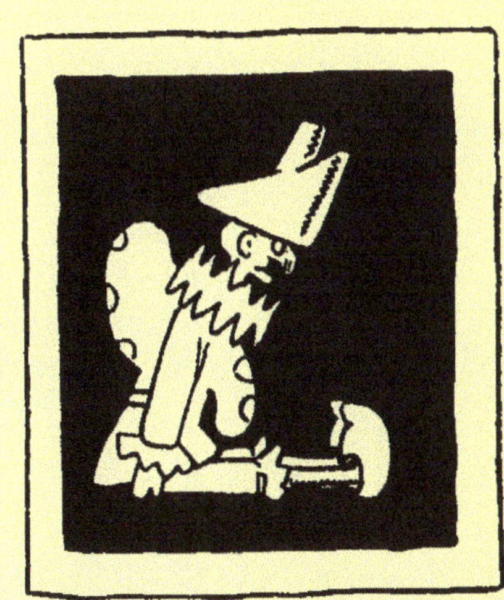

Some camels have one hump, some have two. A camel with one hump is actually known as a dromedary and is most often found in Africa and the Middle East and is known as an Arabian Camel, while a camel with two humps is a Bactrian camel.

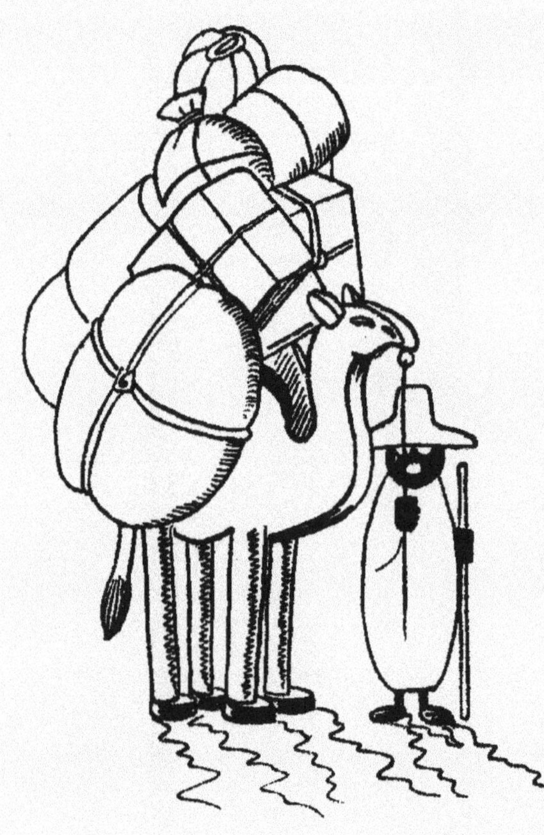

The Arabian camels were considered "a gift from the sky" because of their great strength and endurance.

Big caravans of camels carry bags and treasures on their backs as they walk in the desert. Their big humps hold fatty tissue which they turn into water and food to help them last for days at a time in the hot sun.

This is why camels are also called The Ships of the Desert.

Sometimes, the camels can get lost. But after a long journey, they usually arrive at an oasis where they can eat, drink, and rest.

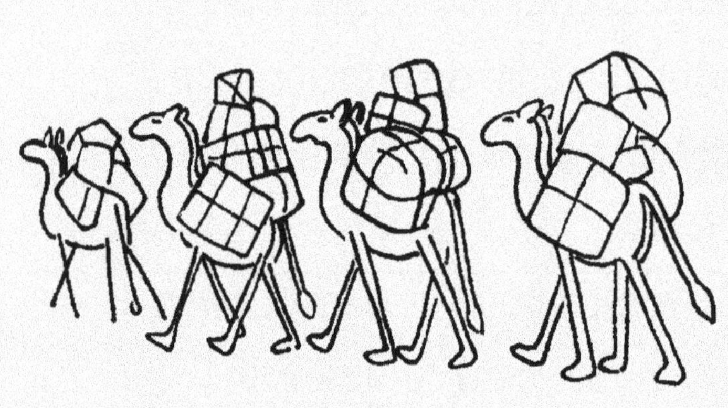

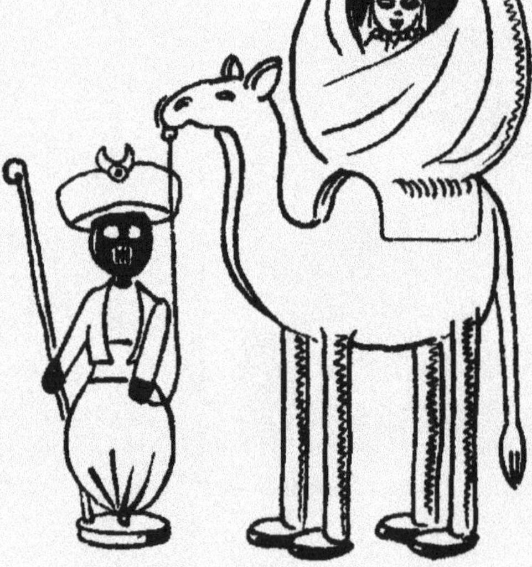

L'AUTRUCHE

(The Ostrich)

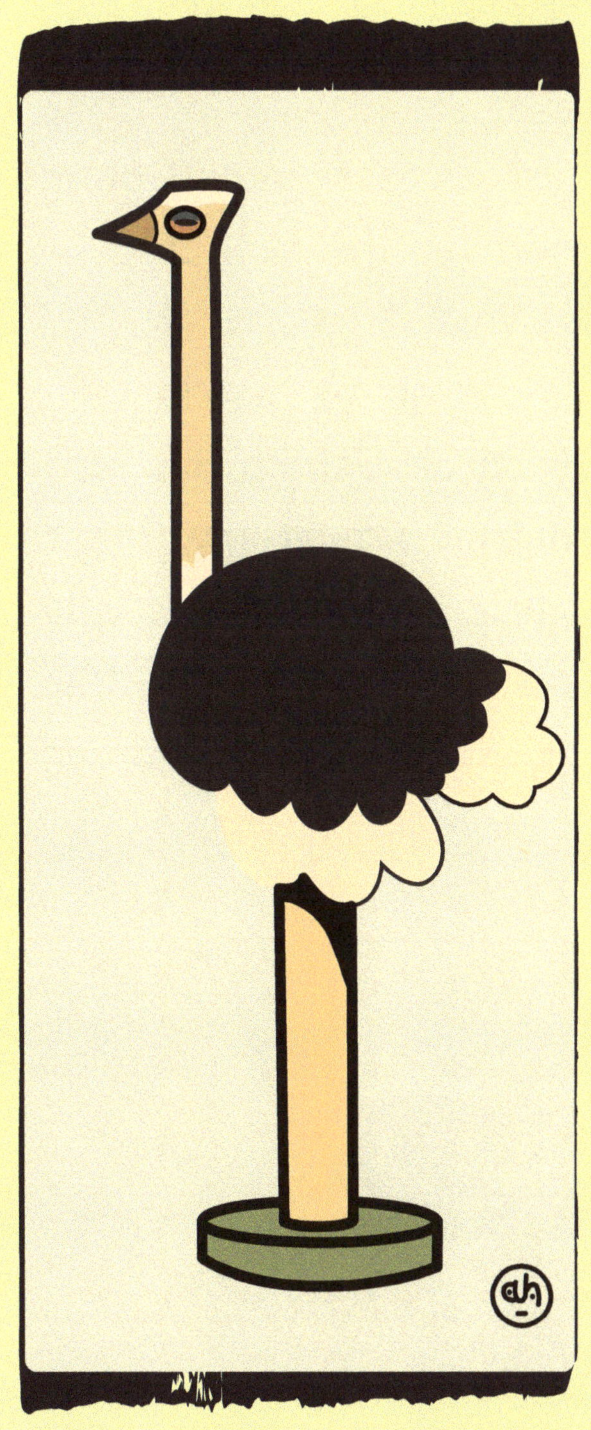

The ostrich is one of the largest birds on earth. Like the penguin, it is flightless, and they run instead of fly. They have very long legs and a very long neck. These allow it to walk and run gracefully while reaching incredible speeds.

Ostriches live in groups in Southern Africa, but are often hunted by men trying to sell their feathers. They also populate parts of Australia along with their cousin, the emu.

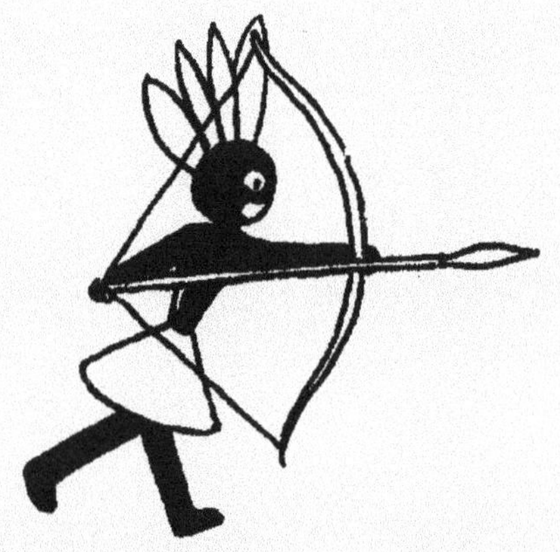

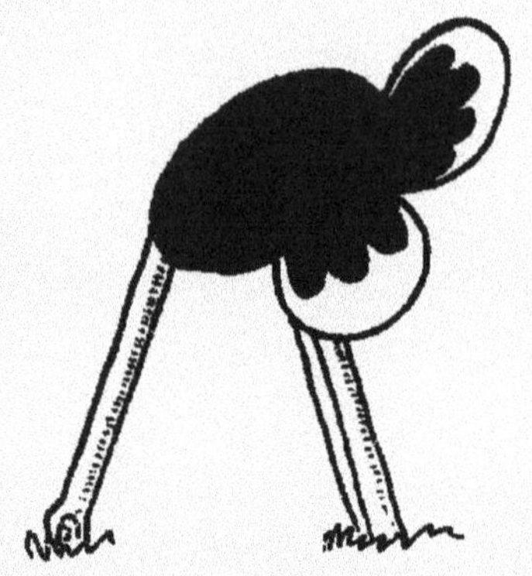

It is not true that when an ostrich is scared It buries its head in the sand! Now remember the Ostrich cannot fly, but it still has wings that it uses while running to make itself faster. It can go so fast that it can win a race against a horse! So an Ostrich has no reason to hide because it can outrun almost any threat!

The Ostrich is huge and because of this, it lays very big eggs. The eggs are so big that they are almost the size of soccer balls! These eggs are very popular around the world, and are considered a delicacy by many.

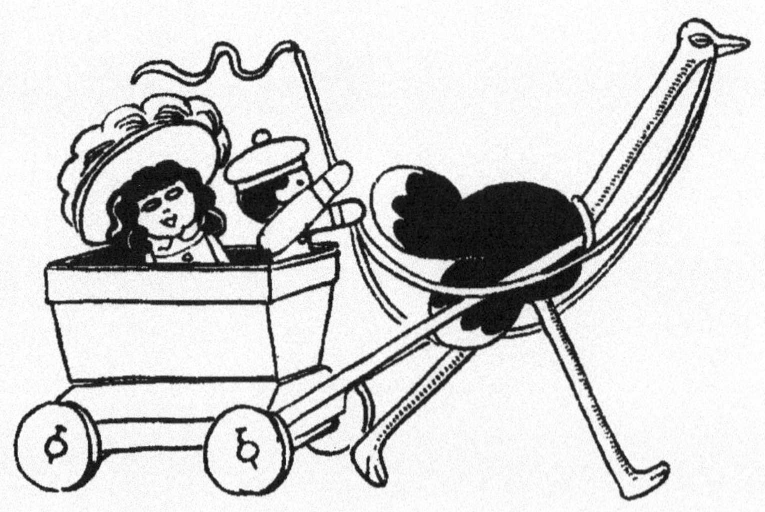

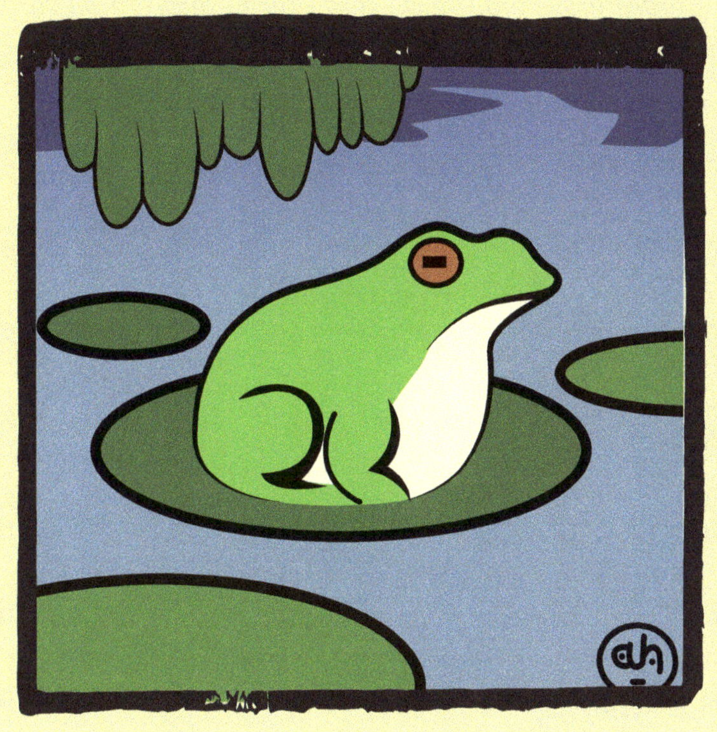

LA GRENOUILLE

(The Frog)

The frog is a lively, dapper fellow who lives in many places around the world. Some might say that the frog looks like a fat gentleman in a vest with wide eyes.

During the winter the frogs usually like to hide and stay under stones. When summer comes, the frogs warm up their bodies and start to croak and sing in the pools and ponds. Hiding among the reeds, the frog catches insects for food. They have long tongues and big mouths that help them catch these dinners.

The frog is much smaller than most other animals so when it hears a step or sound, it jumps to hide. The best hiding place is in the water where the frog can completely disappear. When it jumps, it makes full use of its long hind legs. People often enjoy eating frog's legs. They are cooked in various ways and are used in very fancy restaurants and family dinners alike.

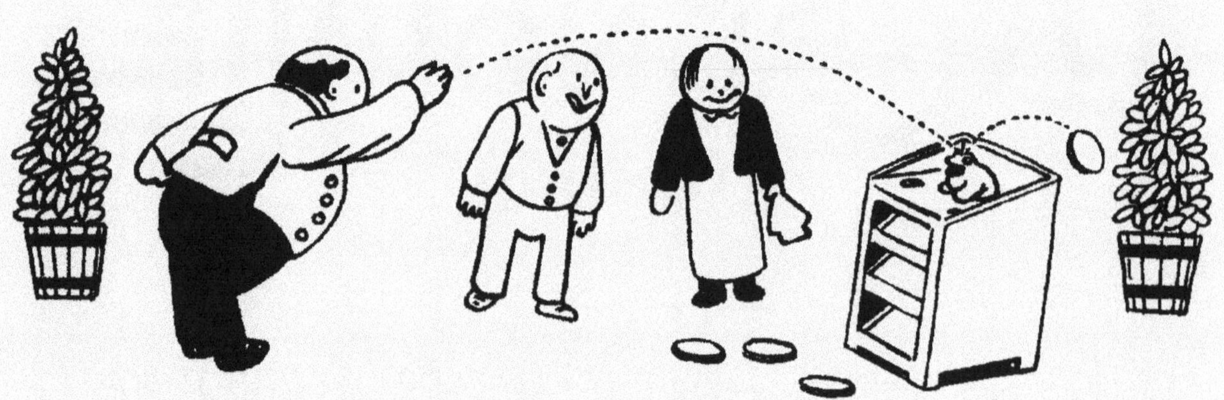

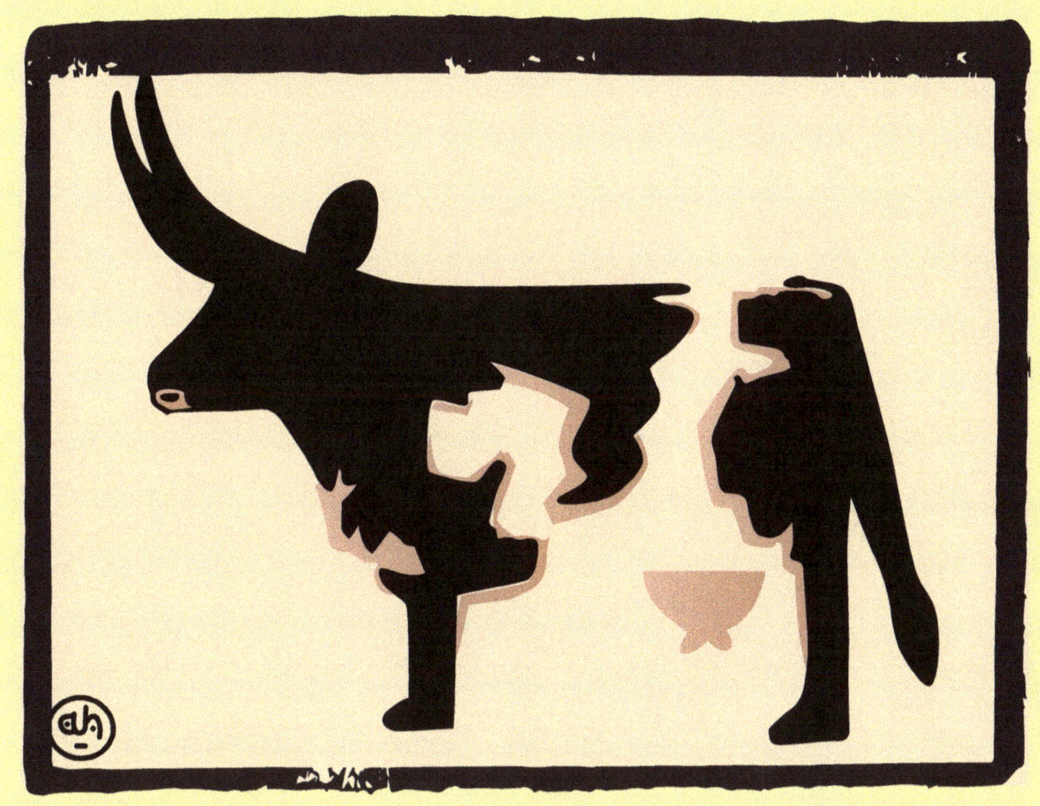

LA VACHE

(The Cow)

The cow is a farm animal. whose milk provides delicious, healthy food.. Cows have two horns on the top of their heads, though they do not really use them. Some of the horns can be really long, as long as a farmer's arm, and some can be smaller, like the size of a hand.

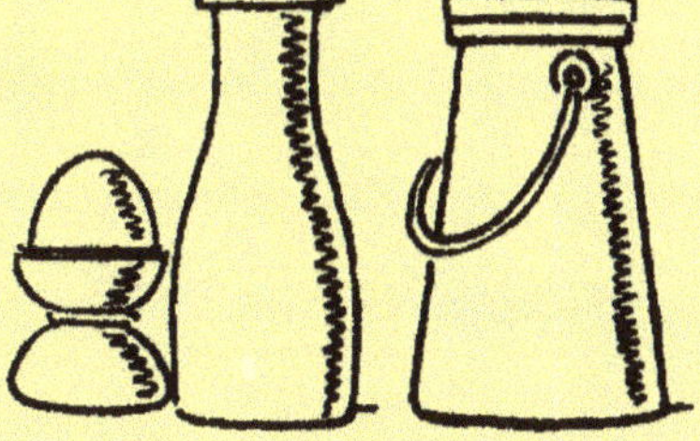

The cows enjoy watching their baby calves play together on the grass where they graze. They have big eyes but tend not to see very well. When they take a deep breath and let out a loud "moo", it is usually to call the herd in for dinner.

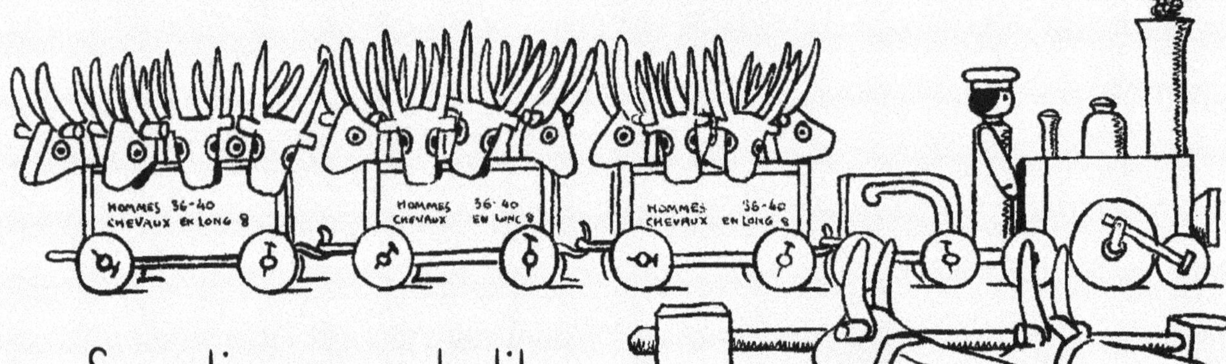

Sometimes people like to raise cows. Then, when they are big and strong, they are sold to other farmers and ranchers. Cows have other uses besides making milk.

Some cows are raised solely as livestock for meat, which is where we get things like steak, hamburger and other things like leather goods.

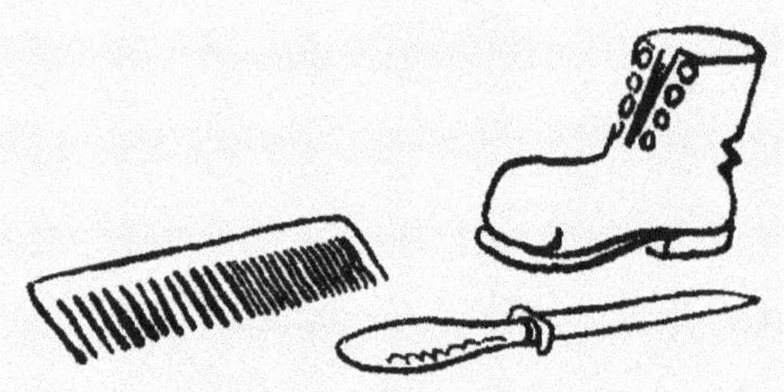

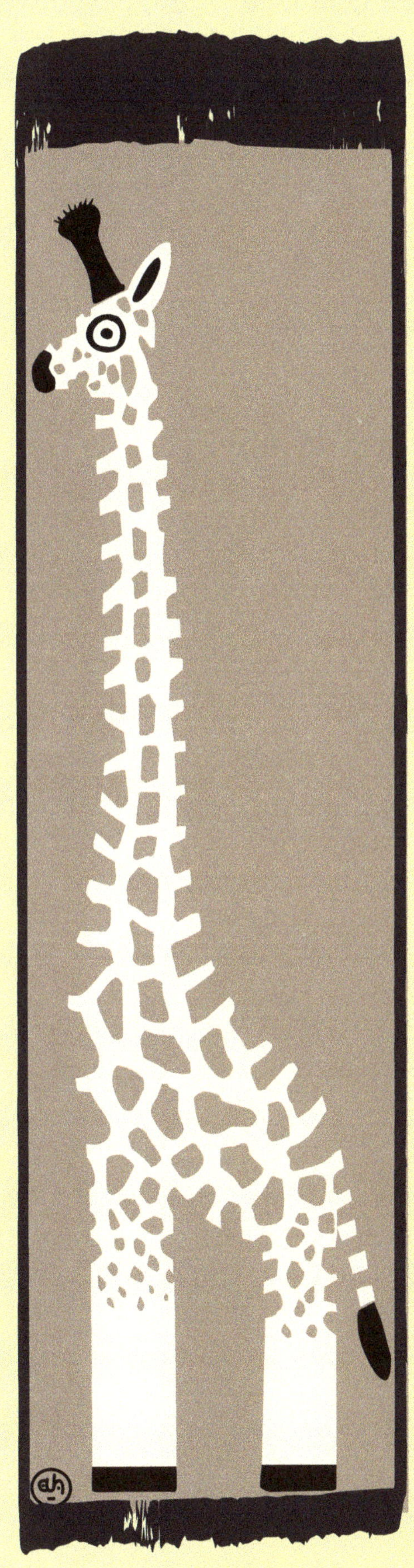

LA GIRAFE

(The Giraffe)

The giraffe is the tallest living animal. It is bigger than lions, bears, and other animals. But instead of being scary, it is actually gentle and harmless. It lives in the African plains where it eats the leaves from tall trees

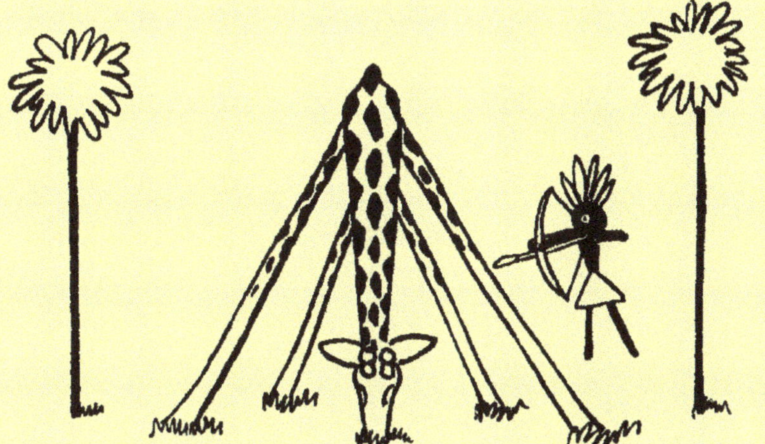

that most animals cannot reach. This is because it is difficult for the giraffe to eat the grass on the ground. We do not know if

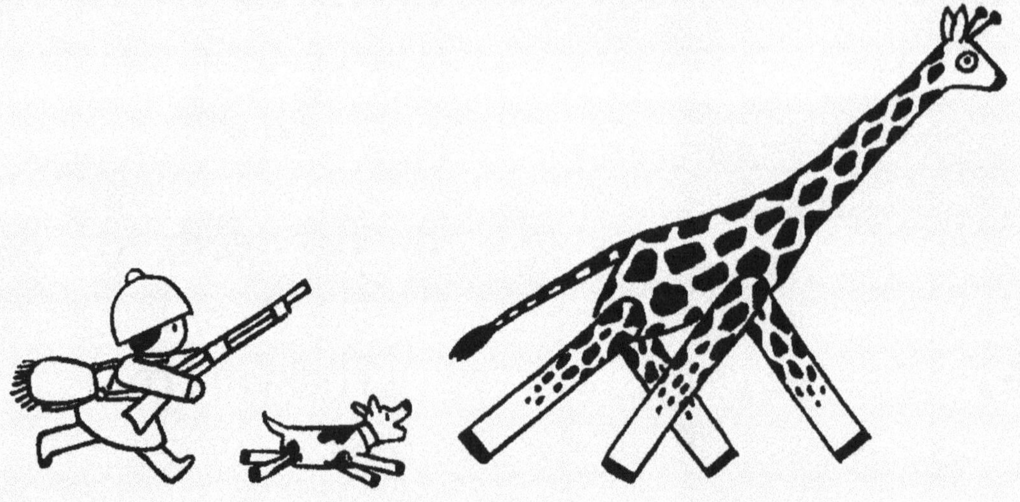

the Giraffe's neck has always been that long.

Some say that it's because the Giraffe kept stretching and reaching for the leaves so much that its neck just kept growing! Many people think the giraffe looks silly with its huge neck and legs and its small head and anxious eyes.

Especially with the two small horns on the top of its head. No one knows why they're there, the horns are harmless and seem to have no purpose. Giraffes are protected animals since they used to be over-hunted. Now they live safely as they run in the wild and eat from tall trees.

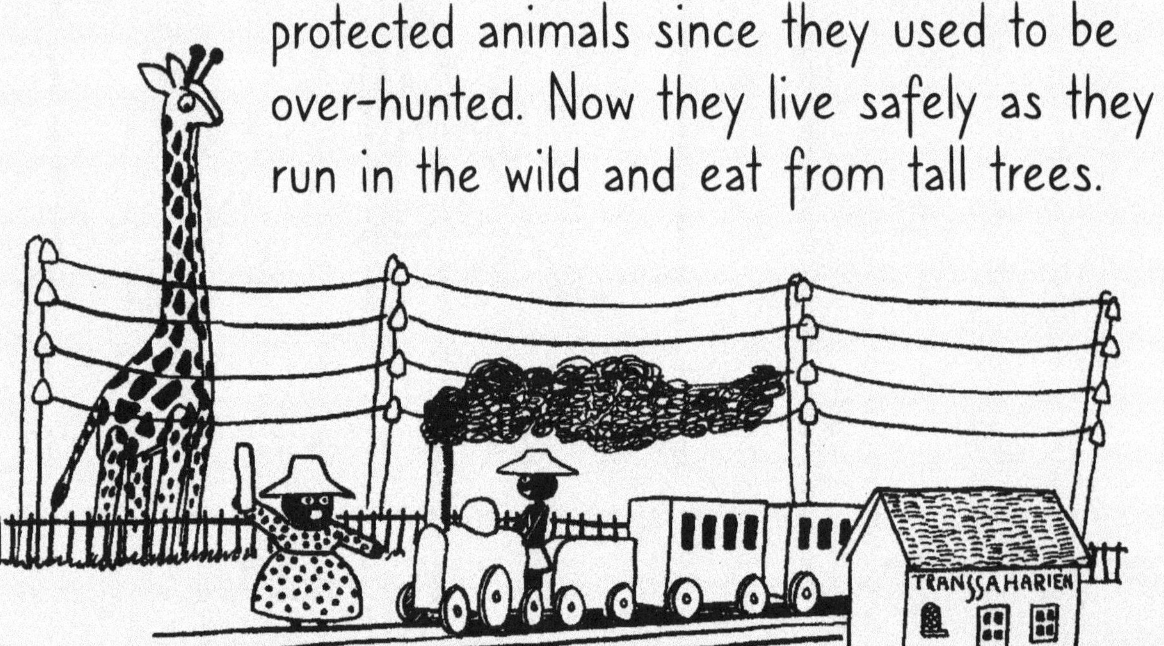

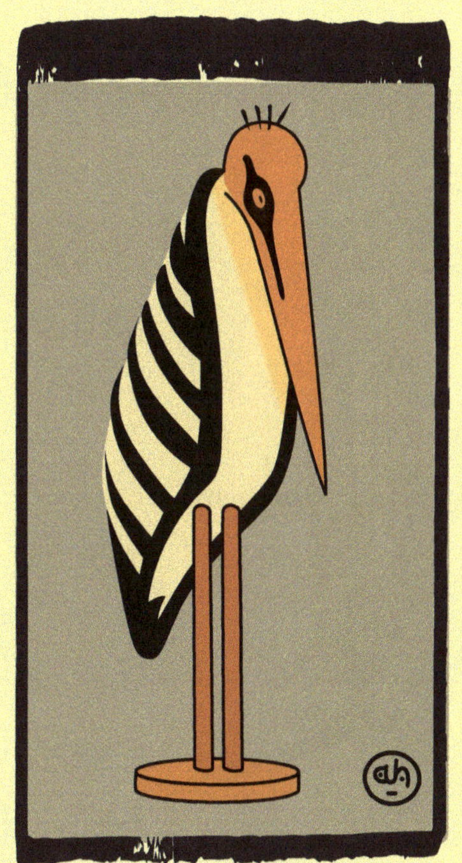

LE MARABOUT

(The Marabou)

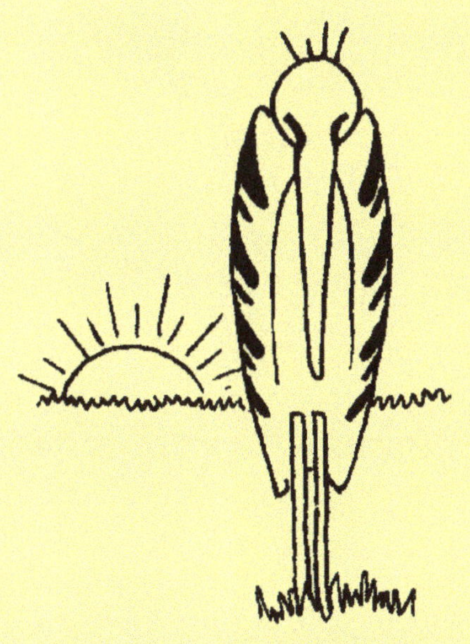

The Marabou is a bird that lives in Africa and Southern Asia and belongs to the stork family. It has an enormous beak but only four hairs on its head. The wings are also very long on both sides, making them look big when predators come close.

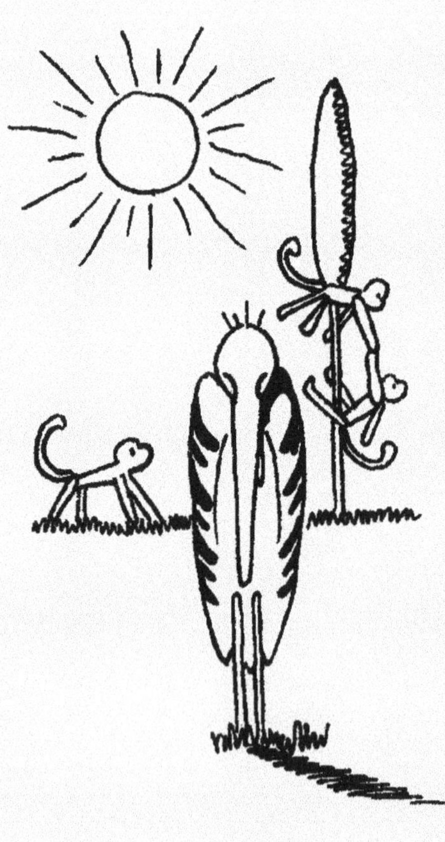

Some people say its colors and patterns make it look like an old gentleman in a suit. The Marabou is ill-tempered and not friendly or a good pet. A scavenger by nature, the Marabou's bare head is like a vulture's head, losing most of its covering from years of sticking their head into the body's of dead animals and digging out the entrails. A full head of hair gets in the way of that kind of scavenging.

Marabous have also been known to eat from human garbage dumps and will put anything in its mouth, including shoes and tin cans.

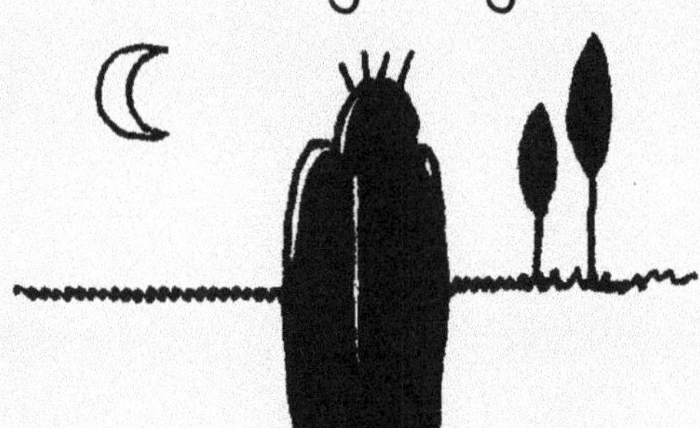

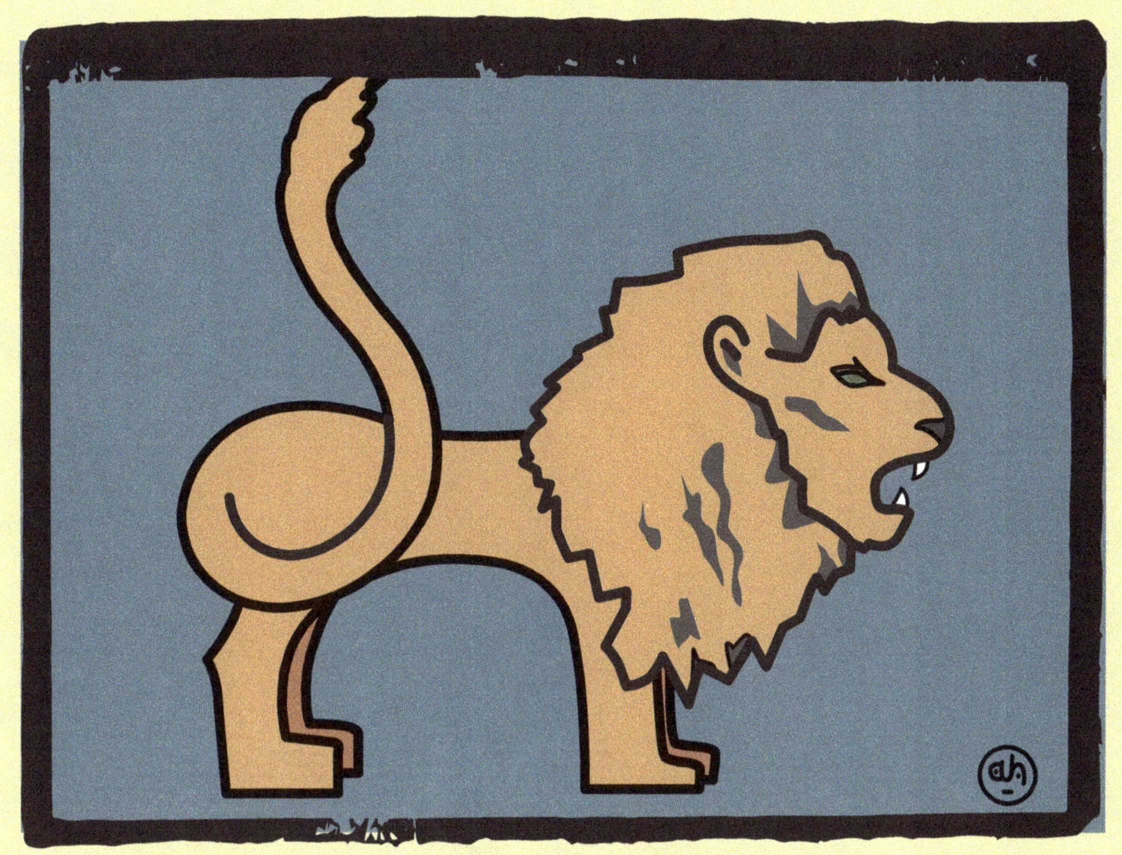

LE LION

(The Lion)

The lion is sometimes called The King of the Jungle. A member of the feline family, its head is covered

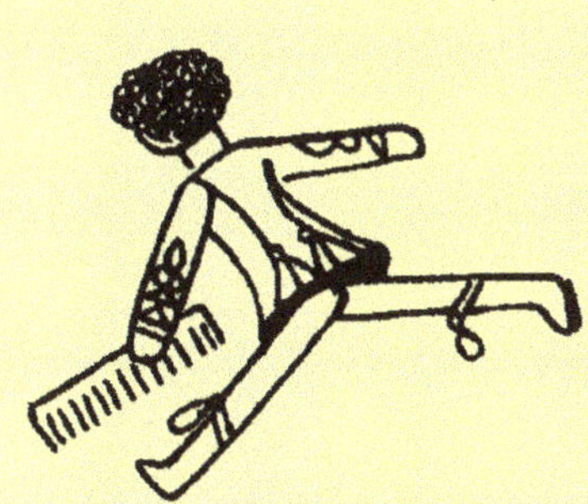

by a huge thick mane of hair. Lions have intimidating yellow eyes and powerful roar.

Lions live in families, or prides, the

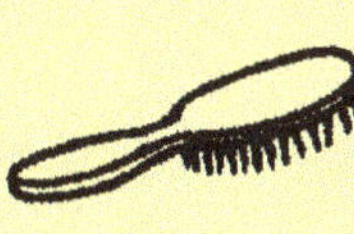

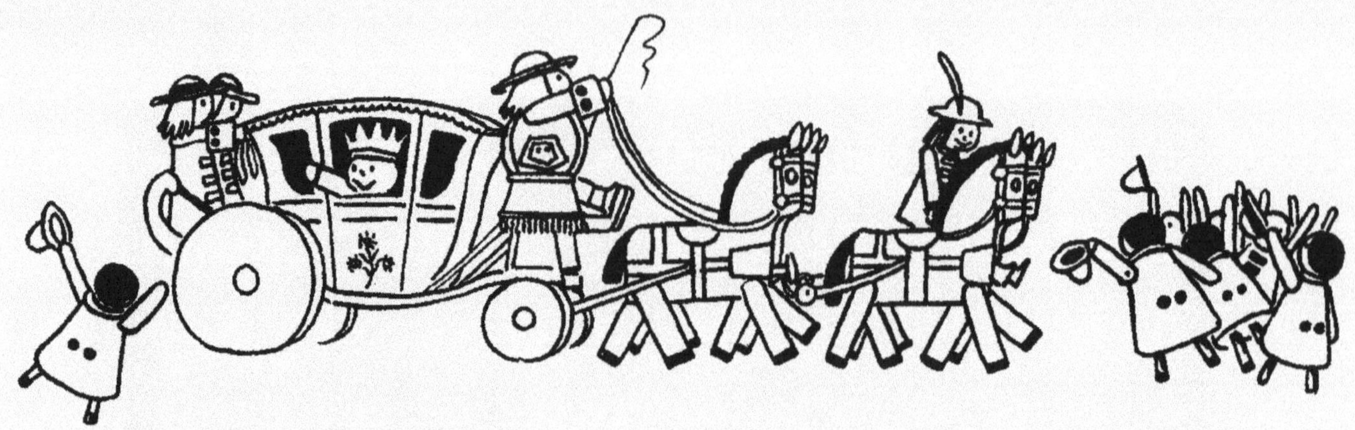

father overseeing the group while the mother lionesses hunt for their food in a large packs Lion's bodies are strong and their teeth are sharp. The roar of the lion is so loud it can wake a sleeping Elephant almost a mile away. A wild lion is able to scare off every other animal around it, or anything that is afraid of being attacked.

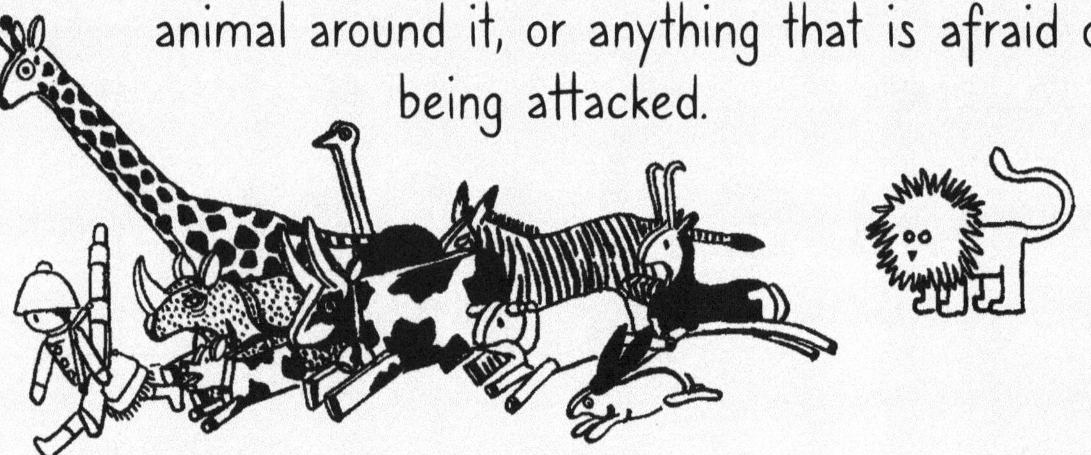

Some men do not fear the lion and are courageous enough to face him, but only when he is stuck in a cage behind iron bars.

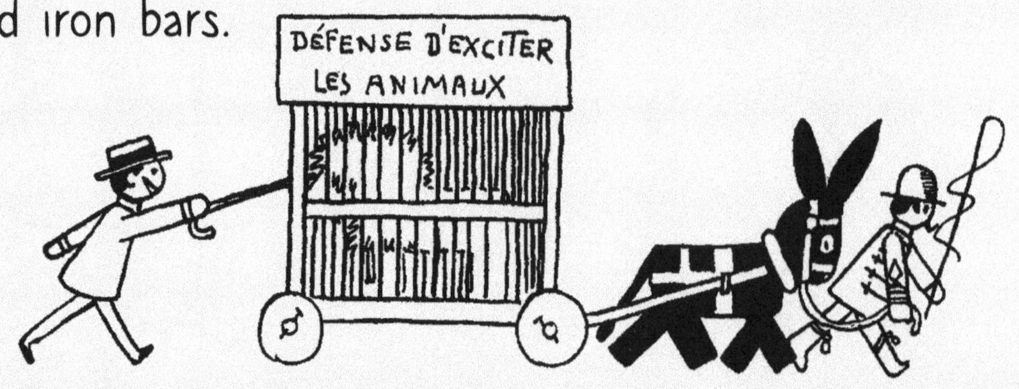

L'OISEAU DES ÎLES

(The Island Birds)

Our ancestors called them the "birds of the island." Sailors brought them over from Africa to America, or "Oceania." Back then, these continents did not have a name so the people said these sailors were returning from "the islands".

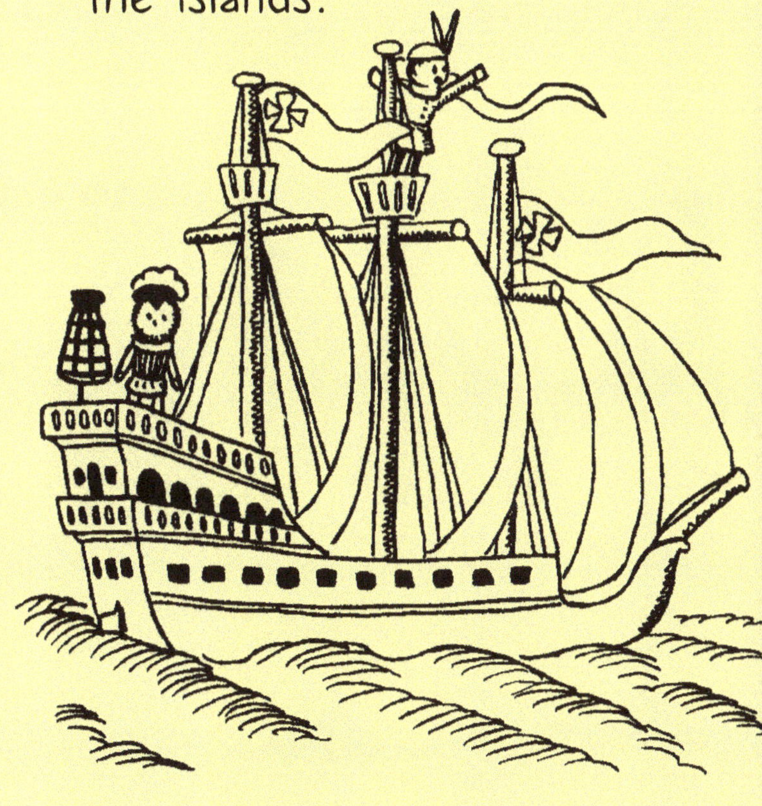

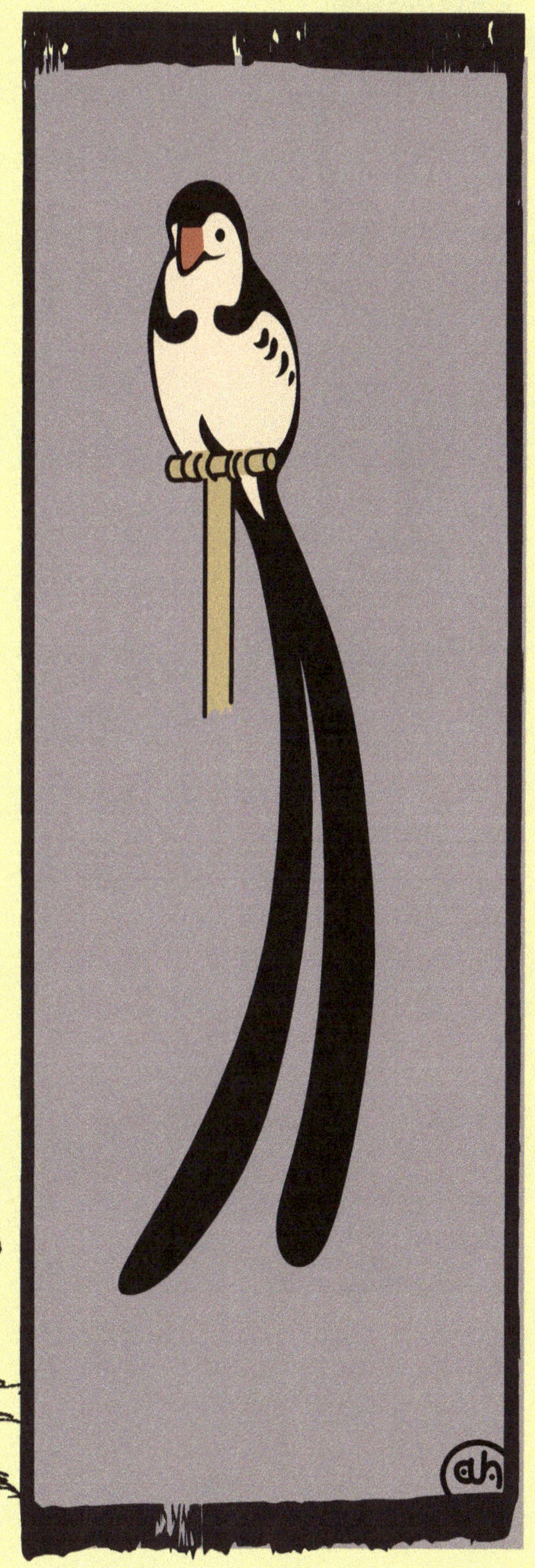

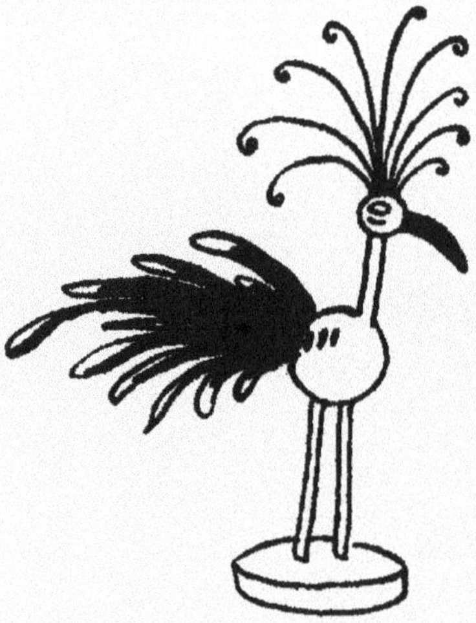

At the time, these birds proved the existence of distant lands, inhabited by mysterious people and fantastic animals.

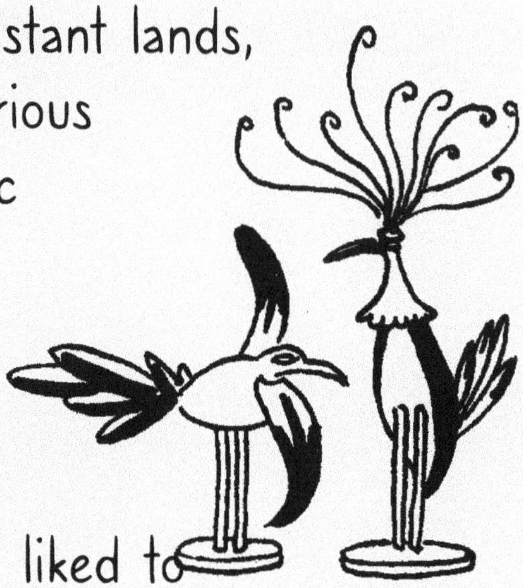

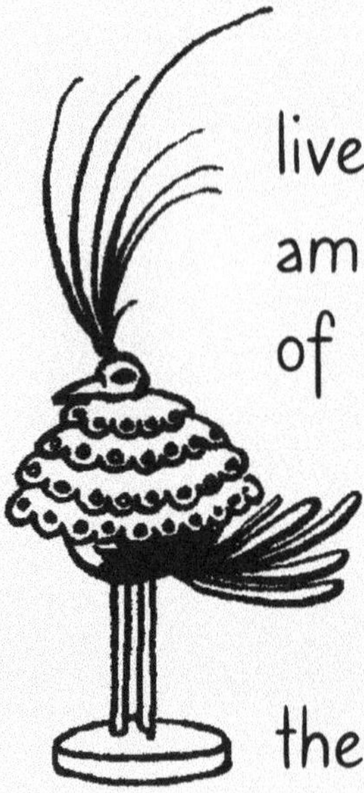

These birds live in warm countries, among shining flowers of many colors. Humans liked to dress them up in rubies, topaz, sapphire, and emerald. Their beautiful tail is by far the longest part of their body. Sadly, these tail feathers were often plucked to make hats for the rich and famous.

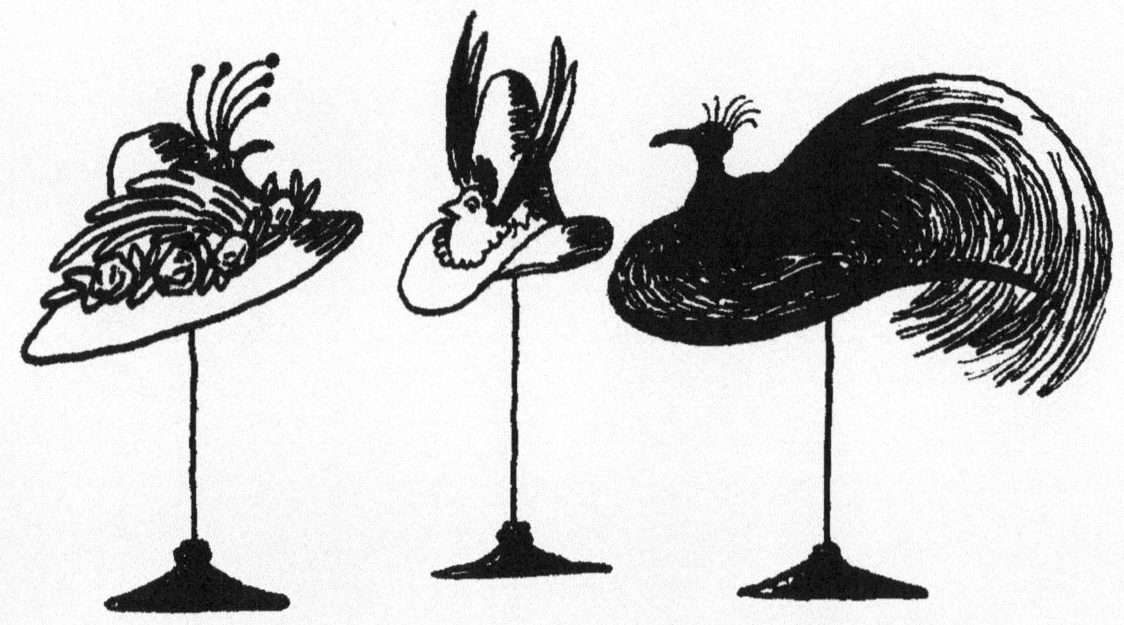

L'OIE

(The Goose)

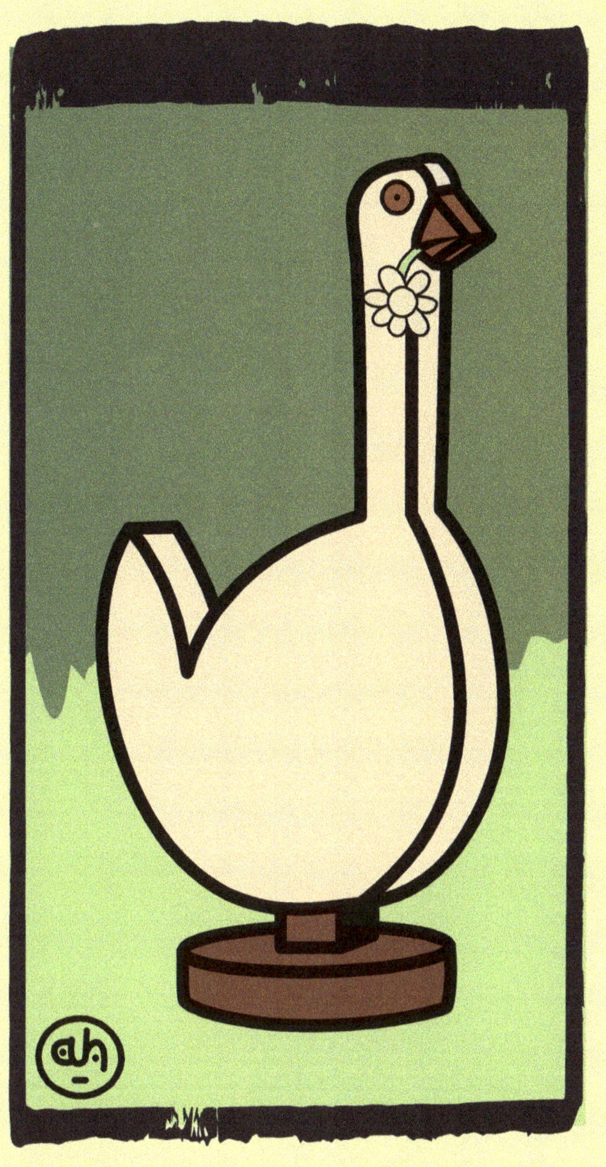

You may have heard someone say, "This person is a silly goose!" But don't say that to a goose because this would make them angry. These birds are far from silly and actually quite smart. When they walk, Geese waddle with their big belly forward, looking serious and confident. When they search for places to live, they look for the lushest meadows with the coolest, shadiest gardens.

Geese make a distinctive honking noises and travel together in groups called "gaggles". Geese are only friendly with each other, and are very protective of their babies. Unfortunately for them, a cooked goose makes a yummy meal. Humans like to use geese in their roasts during the holidays.. Their feathers are also used to make bed-covers and pillows.

The world's most famous goose is, of course,

Mother Goose whose stories have entertained young children for many generations.

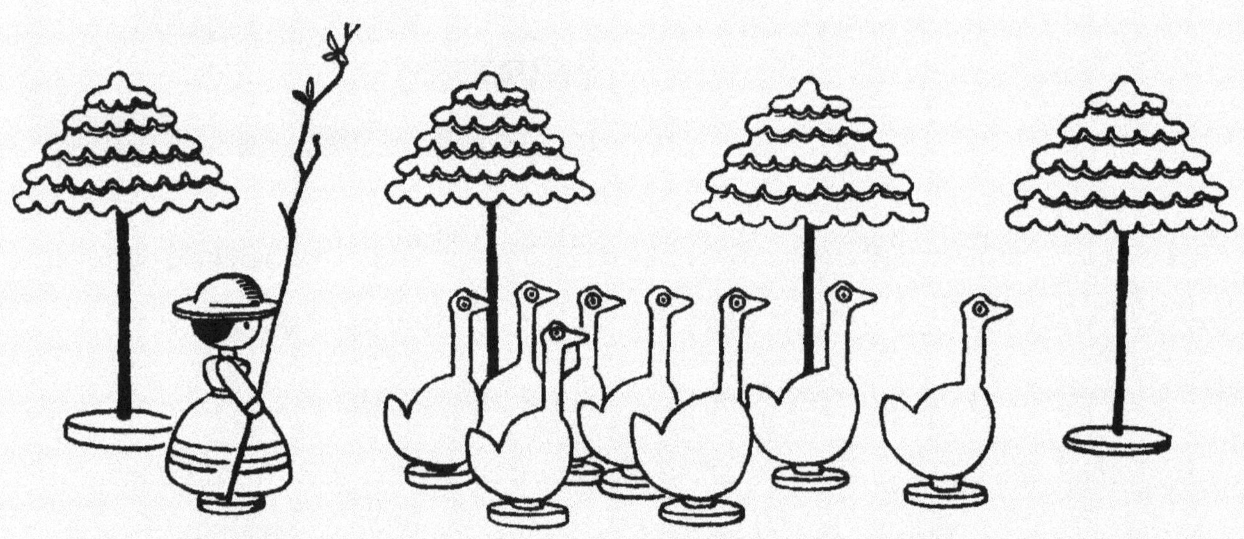

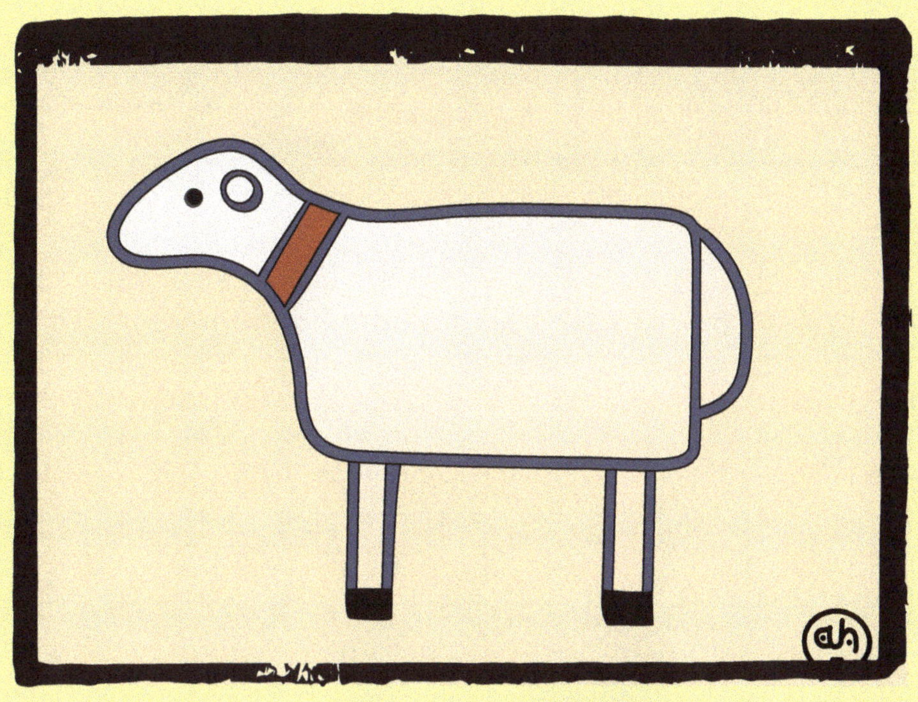

LE MOUTON

(The Sheep)

The sheep is another fun farm animal. It is very gentle and wears a cuddly wool suit. Farmers have to shear them every year to keep them healthy and we then use the wool to make warm clothing.

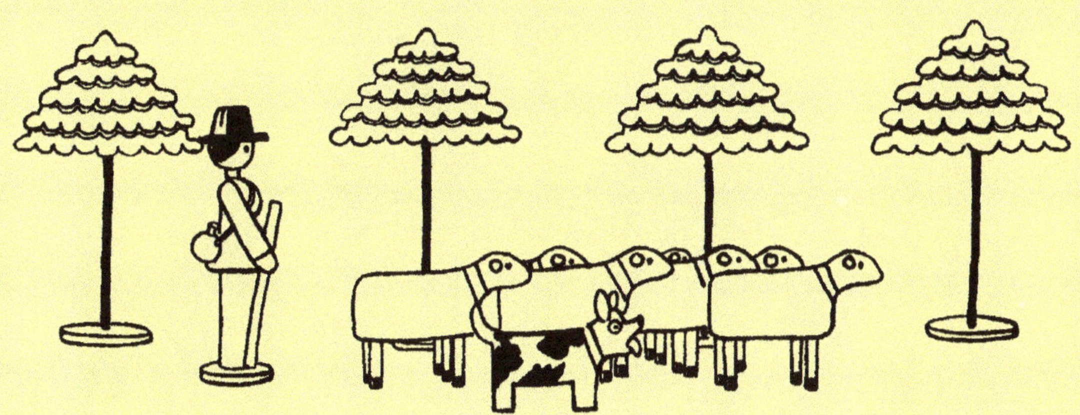

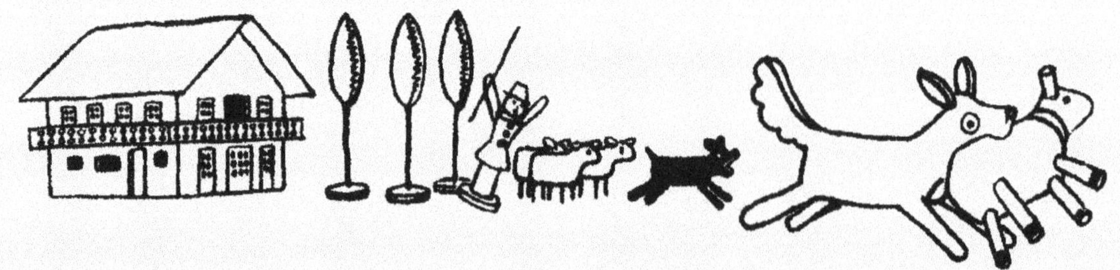

Sheep are very gentle and calm, so gentle that they are unable to guard or protect themselves against animals with sharp teeth and claws, like their legendary enemy the wolf. Because of this, sheep are often guarded by dogs that are trained to lead them in herds and protect them. The baby sheep walking around their mothers are called lambs.

After living a happy and simple life, sheep can also provide us with their meat to eat, some favorites being lamb chops and yummy stews.

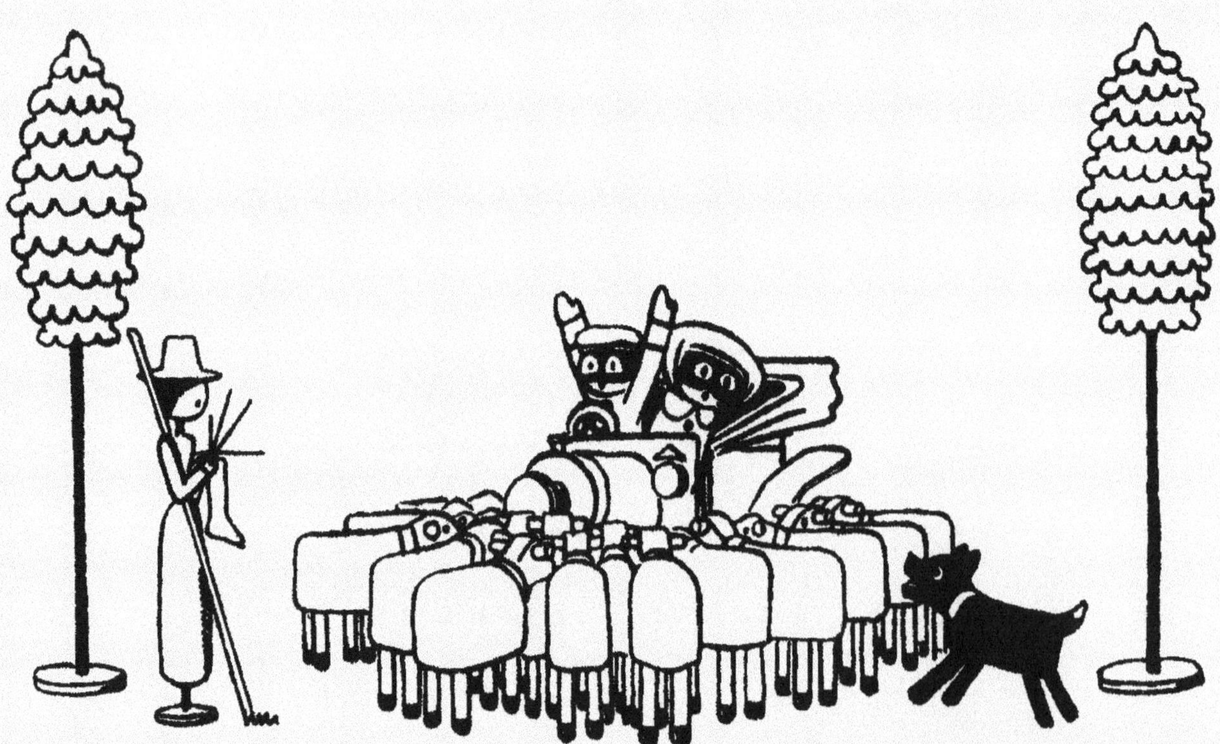

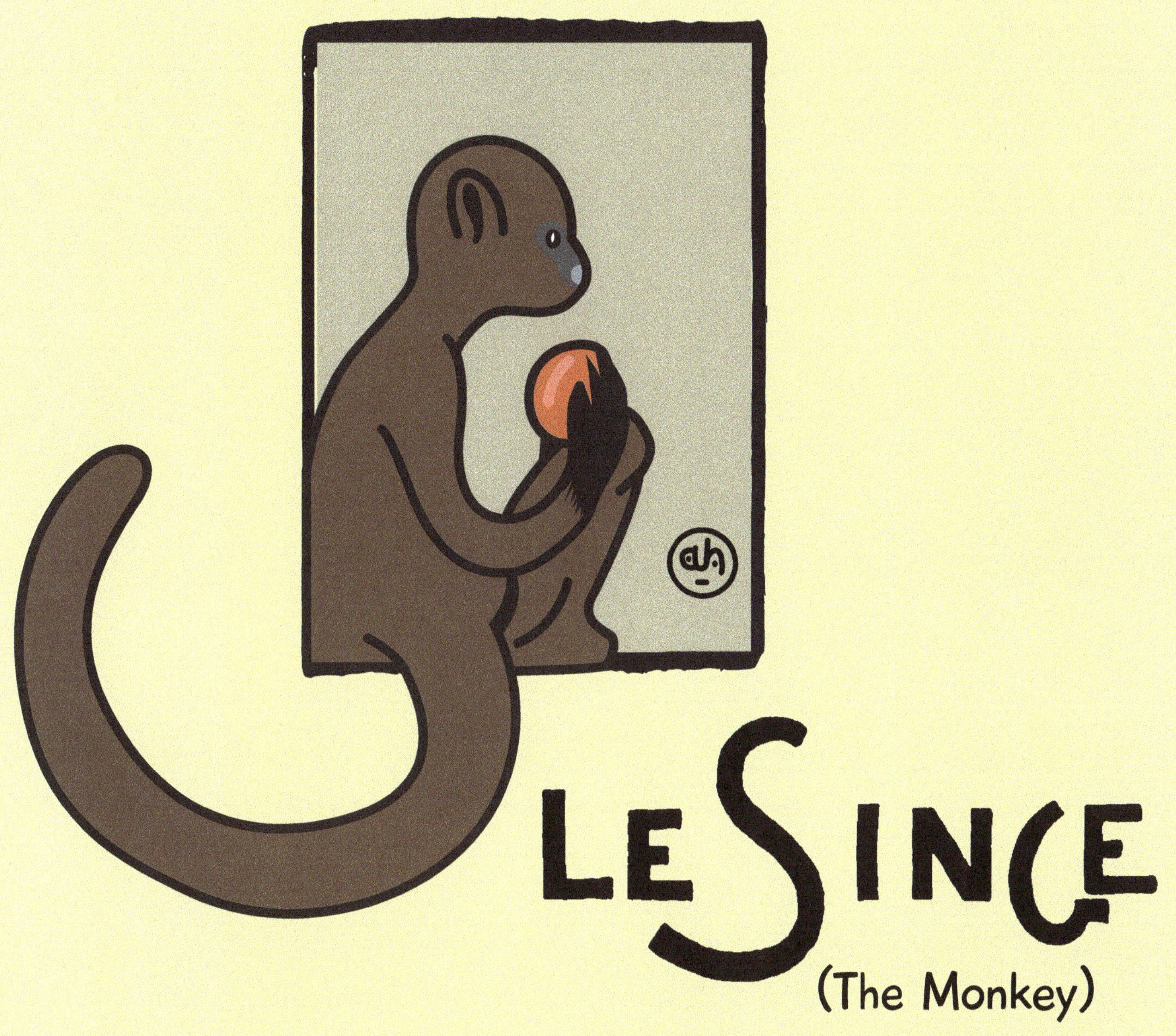

LE SINGE

(The Monkey)

Monkeys can be found in warm and tropical jungles. They live in and swing from the trees and are very mischievous.

They screech, squeal, shout and sometimes it can sound like they are laughing. Monkeys show off their gymnastic skills by moving through the branches and swaying with their hands and their tail. They can climb

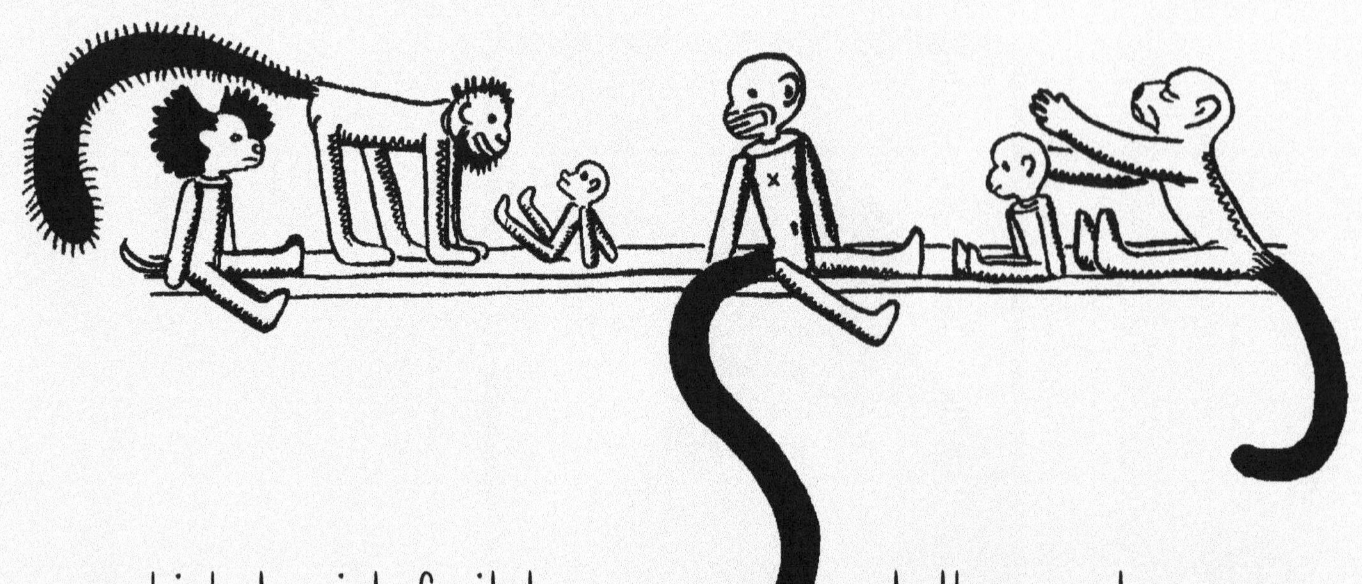

up high to pick fruit to eat; the monkeys sometimes peel the fruit and spit out the pits just like us.

Monkeys can come in a variety of shapes, sizes and colors: some have a painted head in blue and red, others have short hair and some are covered by a thick skin.

These animals are said to sometimes look like humans, even though they can not do everything we can do.

Monkeys are very fast, allowing them to escape from predators. With a leap, or a twirl, the "clown of the forest" can swing far away from its enemies. Once safe, they like to end their stunts by making funny victory faces.

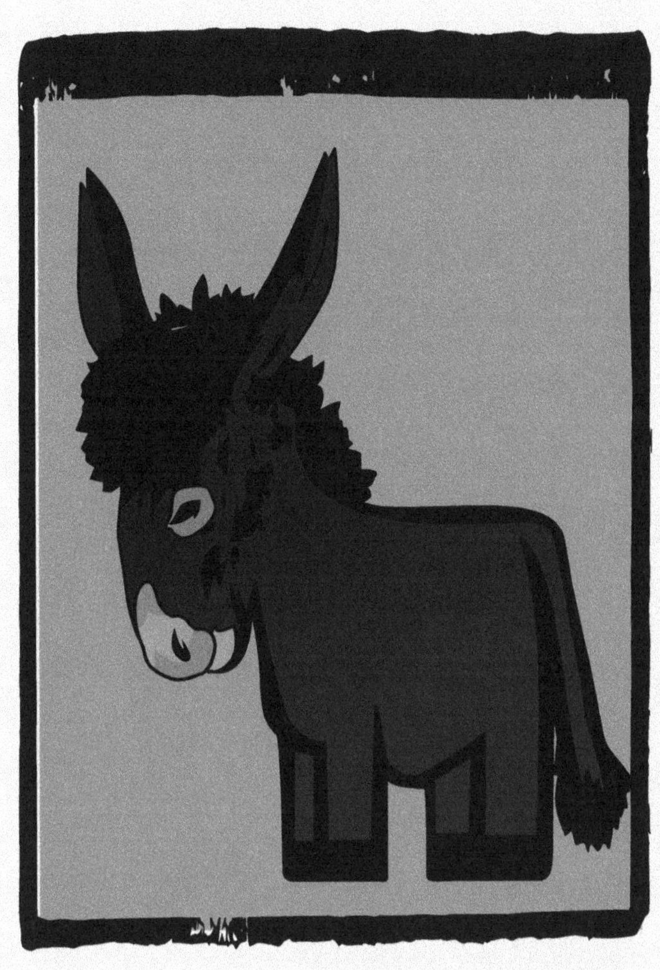

L'ÂNE

(The Donkey)

The donkey is a very patient animal whose purpose is similar to the horse. It is a little smaller than a horse but just as strong. It has a large head and two longer ears. Its thin

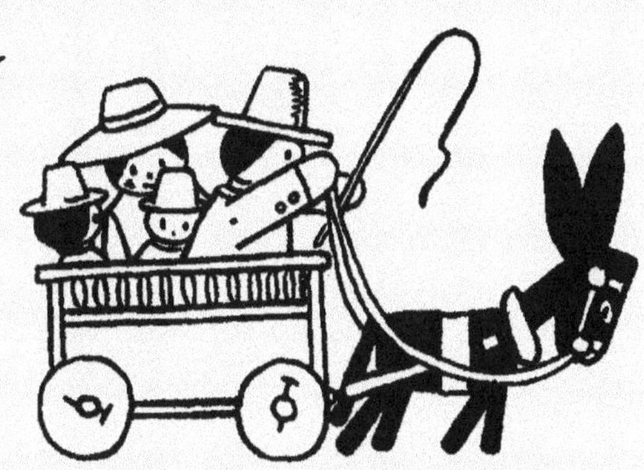

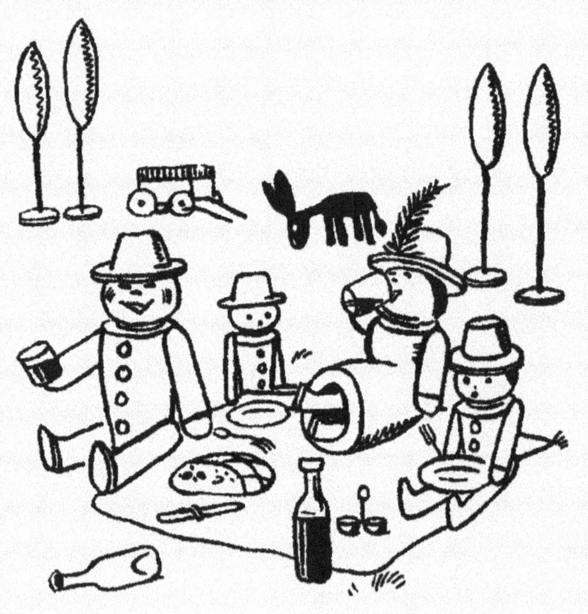

legs have small hooves too.

It neighs loudly when wanting to drink or eat. Out of all the animals, the donkey has the greatest sense of balance. Donkeys can walk along the smallest paths in high mountains without being afraid of falling.

A serious and tough creature, Donkeys can be stubborn, giving them a bad reputation and the perception that they are lazy, or dumb. There are other names for the donkey such as Ass and Jack, and female donkeys are called Jenny's.

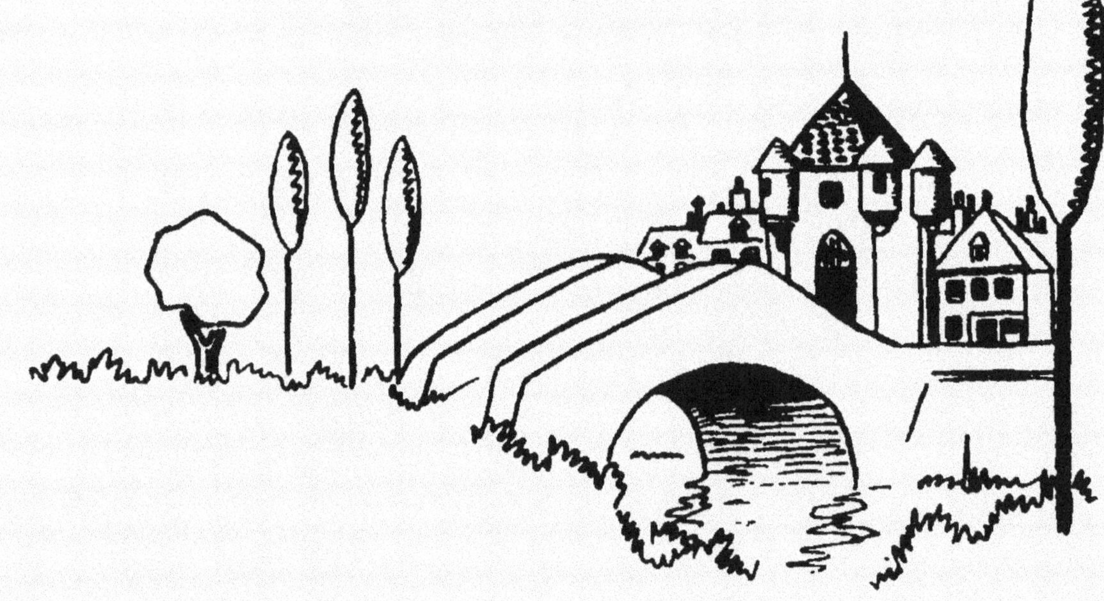

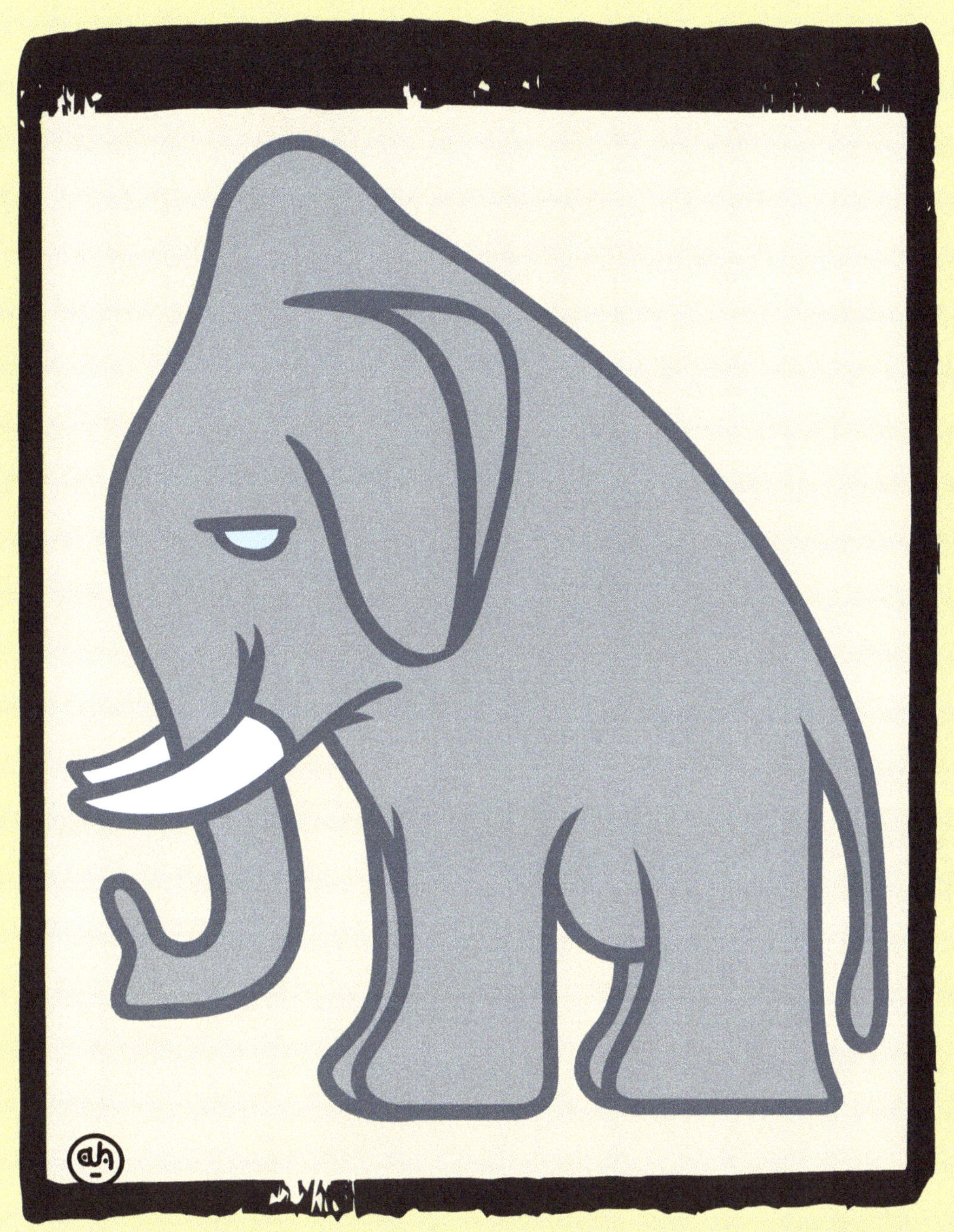

L'ÉLÉPHANT

(The Elephant)

The elephant is the biggest mammal on earth. It has a trunk and two large incisor teeth which grow into tusks.

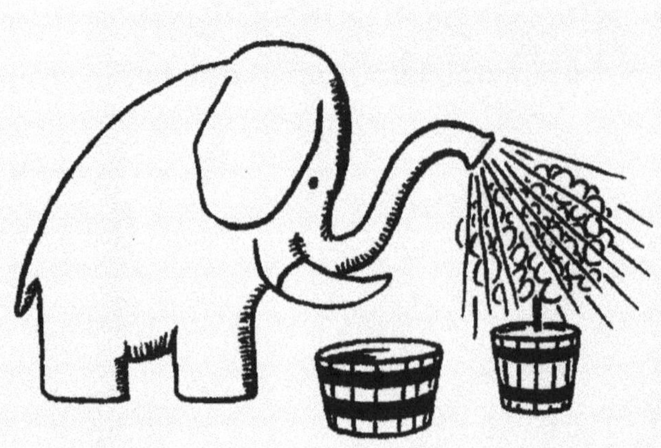

There are elephants in both Africa and Asia. In the wilderness the elephants like to live in groups and eat from the trees. They enjoy playing in the water when the sun is too hot and washing themselves with the help of their long noses called trunks.

Some elephants are domesticated, which means people take care of them. Thanks to the elephant's tame nature, they help their owners and farmers transport heavy items.

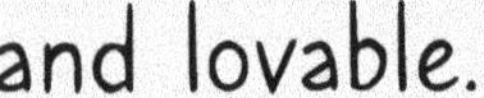

Throughout history, they were used to help fight battles and carry artillery. Many kids love the elephant the most because it is caring and lovable.

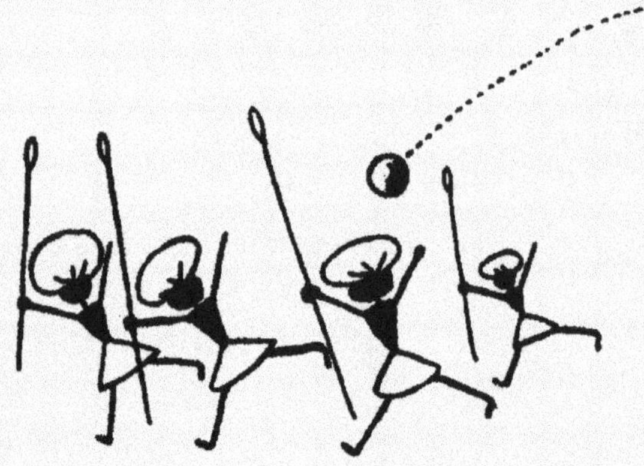

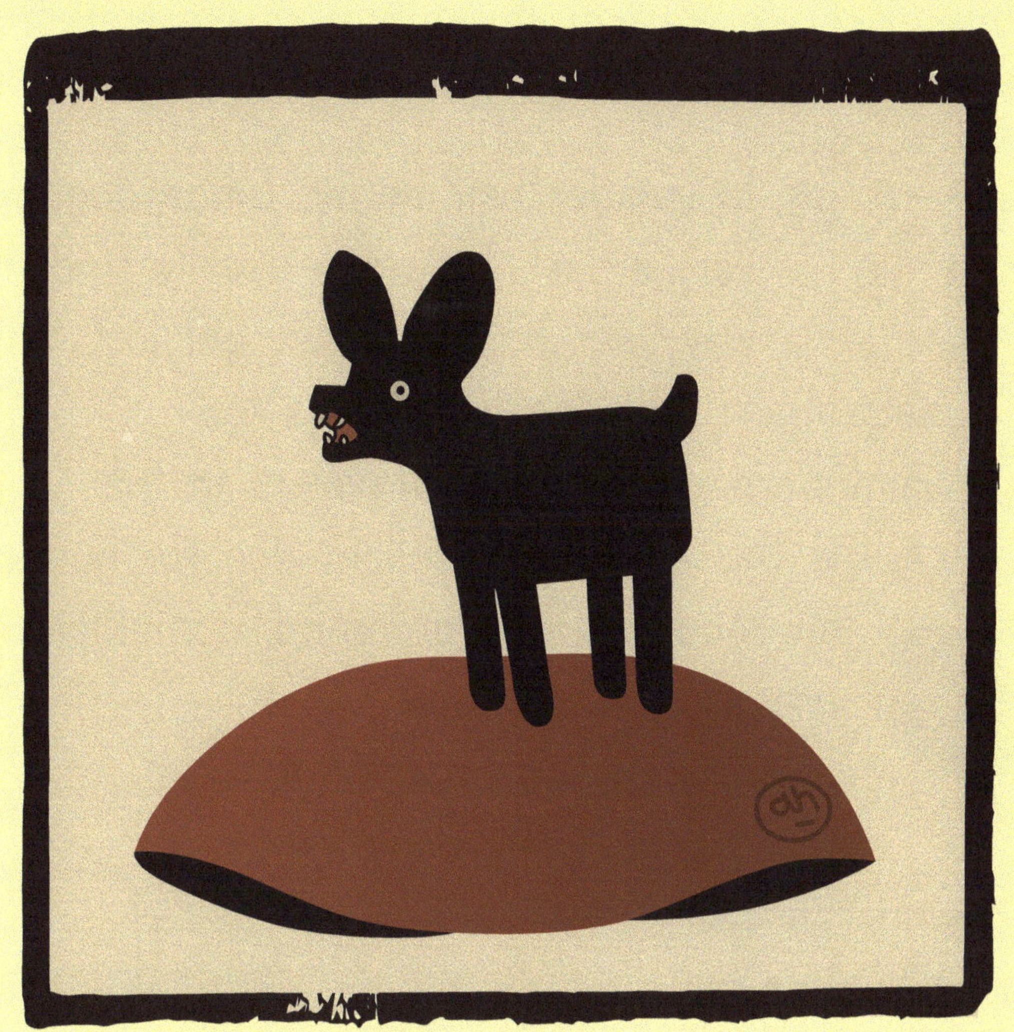

LE CHIEN

(The Dog)

The dog is known as man's best friend and is also the most intelligent domestic animal. The dog enjoys greeting its owner with joy, happiness, and tons of kisses, but it can become furious and protective when strangers try

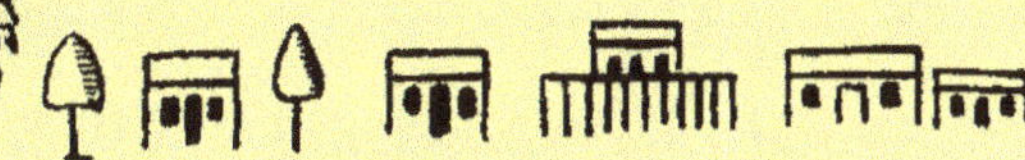

to invade their home. Since dogs are very smart, they can usually find their way back home if they get lost. They tend to help others with locating things too.

The Saint Bernard dog helps travelers in the mountains; the Basset is an excellent dog for hunting; the Poodle can be groomed in multiple ways, some of them funny, earning it the nickname "the clown of the dogs." The Hound can easily catch a wild rabbit while running.

In old times, the dogs were included in military regiments, taking part in war alongside humans. The dogs guarded the camps, but enemy soldiers tried not to harm them.

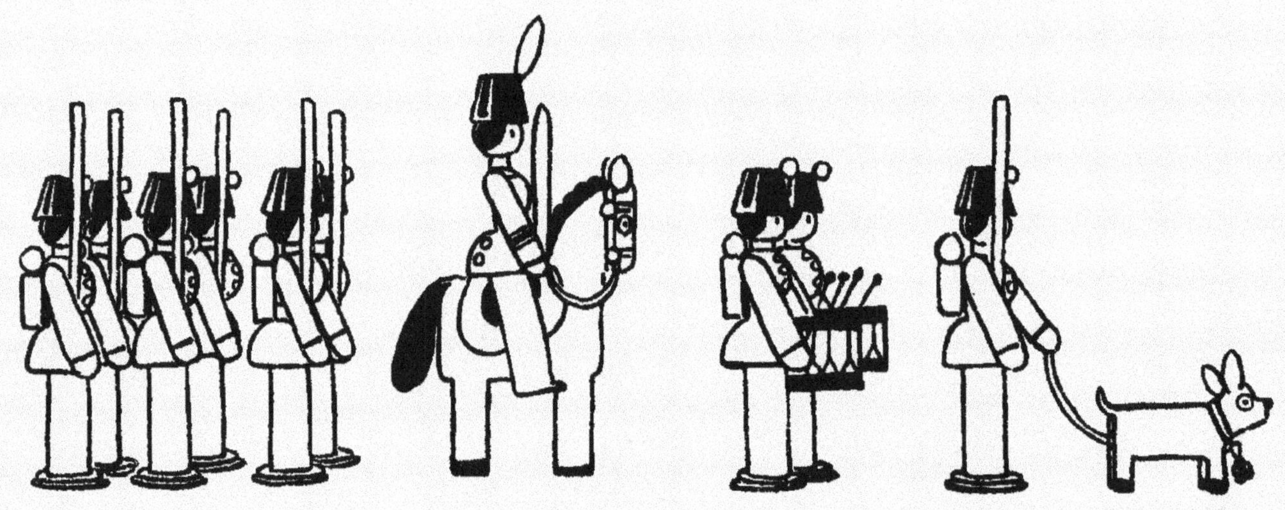

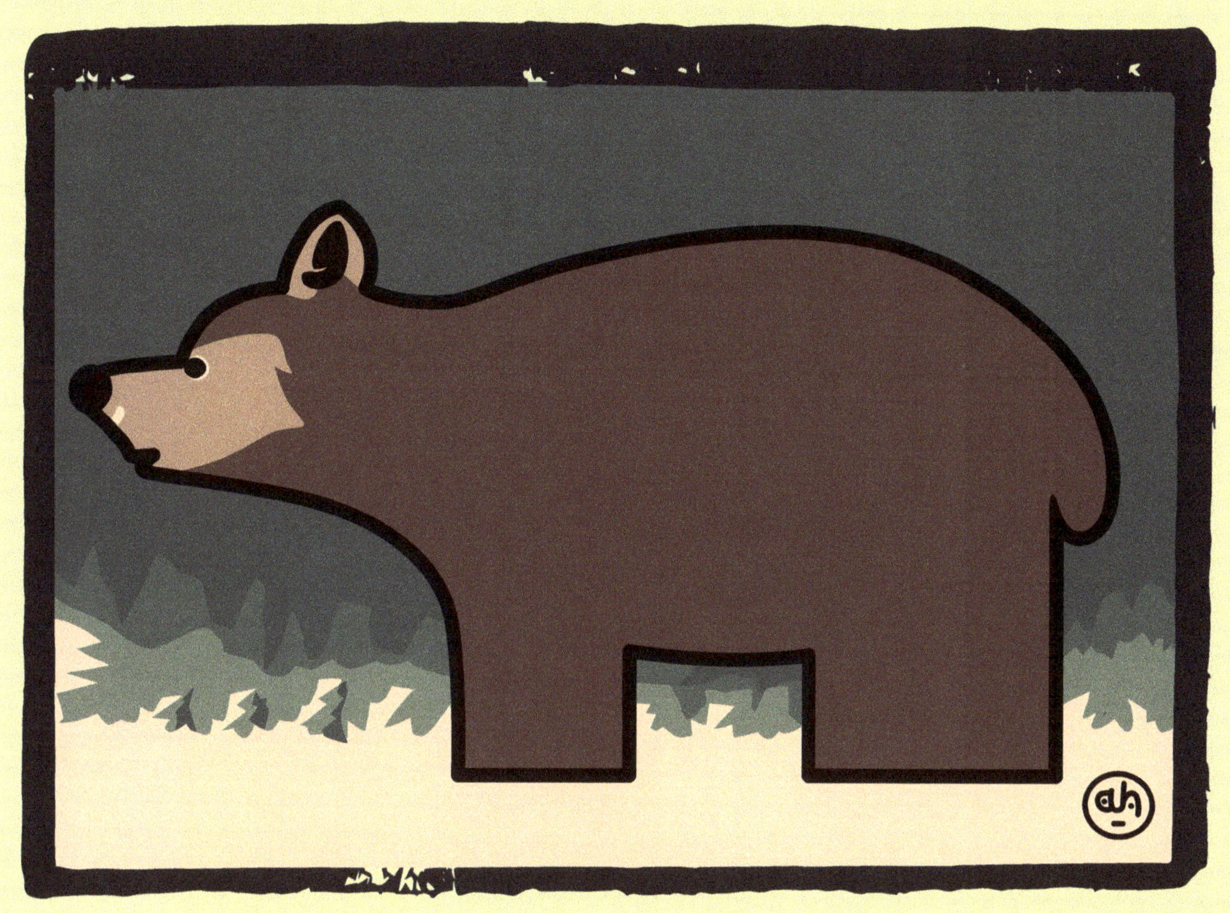

L'OURS

(The Bear)

The bear is a large animal that looks cute and friendly, but unfortunately is not as cuddly as it looks. It lives in mostly northern forested areas.

The bear can have white, brown, or black fur. The white ones are called Polar Bears, since they live near the North Pole. The others are simply named Brown bears and Black bears.

Despite the clumsy appearance, the bear is actually quick and can move very fast.

The bear is hunted for its warm and soft fur, but many people have been injured hunting them.

The bear may be big but it is very sneaky and hard to find. Nevertheless, the bear is an animal that is loved by many, especially children, who love their trademark stuffed teddy bears. Just be careful if you see a real baby bear cub, as their mothers can get viciously protective.

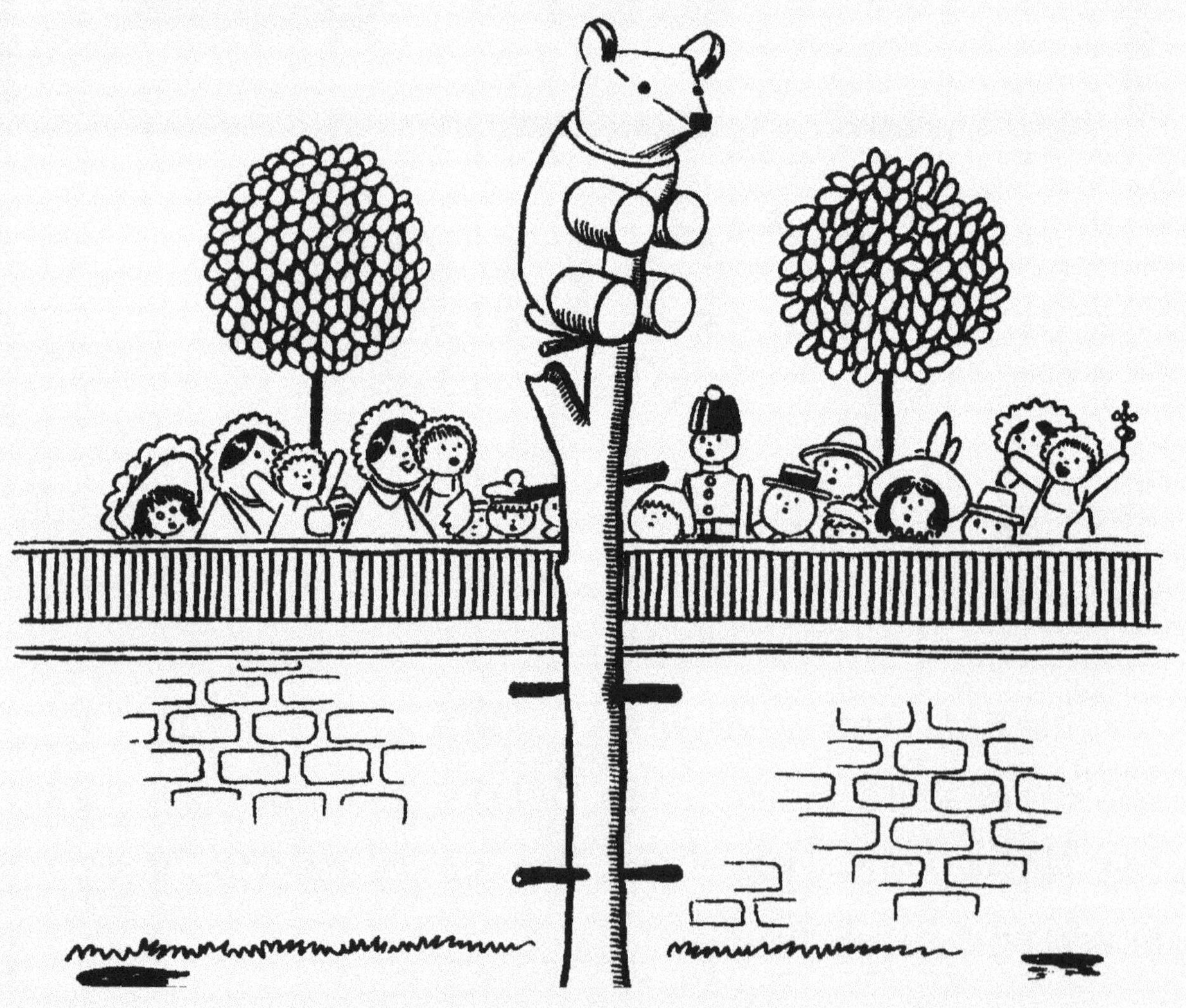

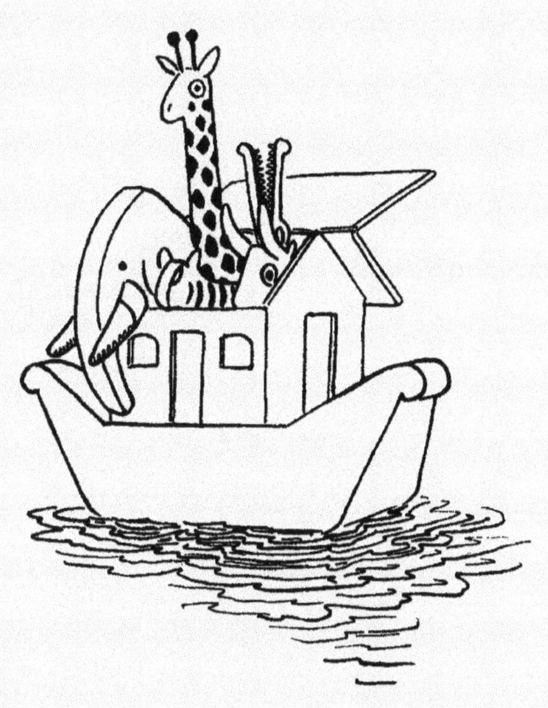

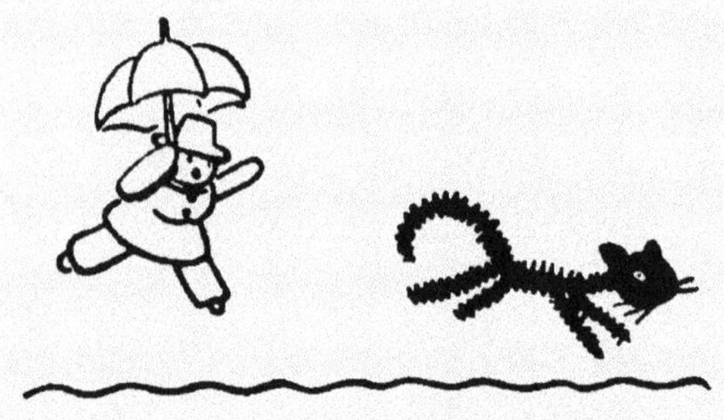

imprimé par

A. TOLMER et Cie

13 QUAI D'ANJOU

PARIS

Other Book Reproductions by SLG Publishing

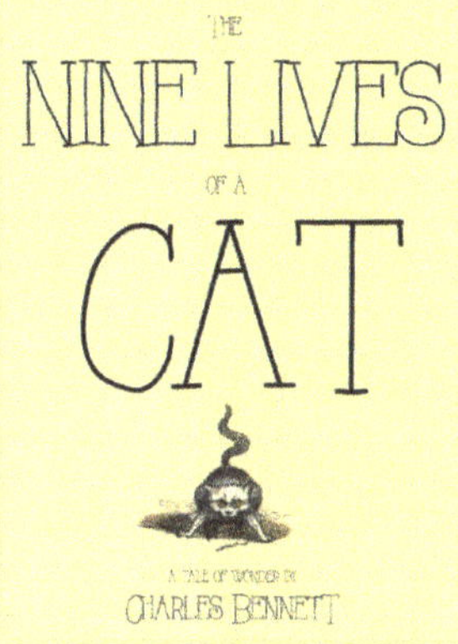

Nine Lives of a Cat
By Charles Bennett
$4.99

Available on Amazon.com and other online booksellers.

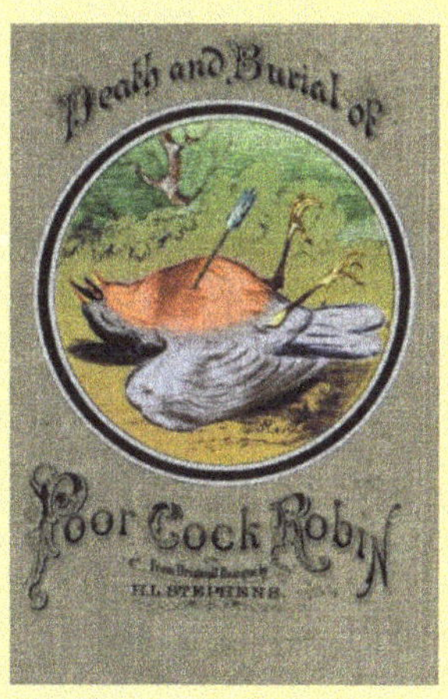

The Death and Burial of Poor Cock Robin
By H.L. Stephans
$4.99

Available on Amazon.com and other online booksellers.

Even more at www.slgpubs.com

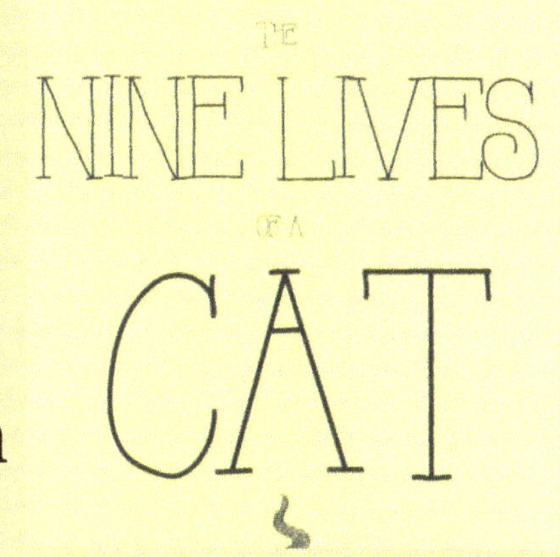

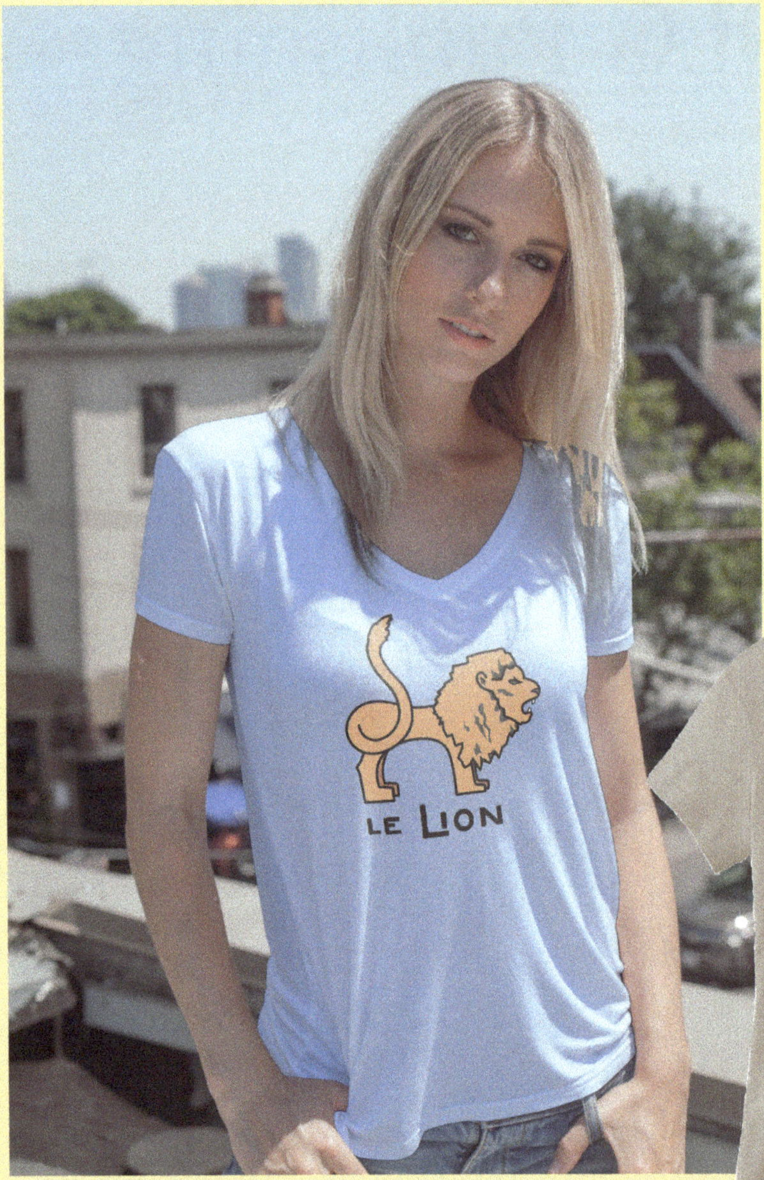

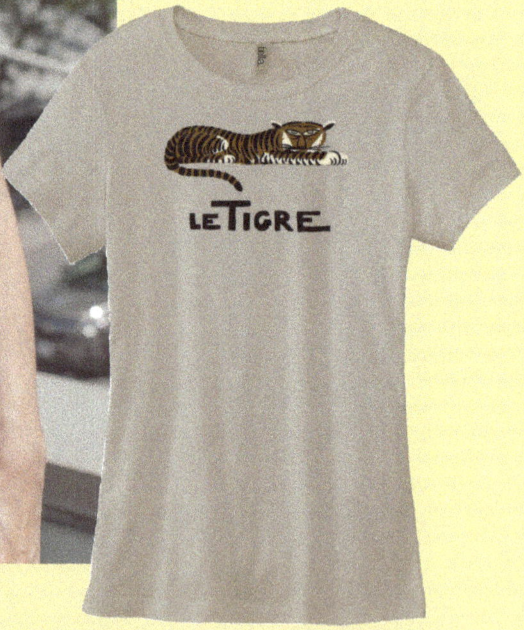

www.ingramcontent.com/pod-product-compliance
Lightning Source LLC
LaVergne TN
LVHW060643110826
845147LV00018B/1028
* 9 7 8 1 5 9 3 6 2 2 9 1 6 *